P9-DEO-050

Neil Postman

The End of Education

Neil Postman was University Professor and Chair of the Department of Culture and Communication at New York University. Among his twenty books are studies of childhood (*The Disappearance of Childhood*), public discourse (*Amusing Ourselves to Death*), education (*Teaching as a Subversive Activity*), and the impact of technology (*Technopoly*). He died in 2003.

Also by Neil Postman

Building a Bridge to the 18th Century

Technopoly

Conscientious Objections

Teaching as a Subversive Activity
(with Charles Weingartner)

Crazy Talk, Stupid Talk

Teaching as a Conserving Activity

The Disappearance of Childhood

Amusing Ourselves to Death

The End of Education

The End
of Education

Redefining the Value of School

Neil Postman

VINTAGE BOOKS

A Division of Random House, Inc.

New York

FIRST VINTAGE BOOKS EDITION, NOVEMBER 1996

The Library of Congress has cataloged
the Knopf edition as follows:
Postman, Neil.
The end of education: redefining the value of school / Neil
Postman.—1st ed.
p. cm.
Includes bibliographical references and index.
ISBN 0-679-43006-7
1. Education—United States. 2. Educational change—United
States. 3. Education—United States—Aims and objectives. I.
Title.
LA217.2.P67 1995
370'.973—dc20 94-46605
CIP
Vintage ISBN: 0-679-75031-2

Random House Web address:
http://www.randomhouse.com/

Printed in the United States of America
79B86

To Alyssa and Claire

Contents

Preface

The last book I wrote entirely on the subject of education was published in 1979. I return to the subject now, not because the education world has suffered from my absence, but because I have. I began my career as an elementary school teacher and have not for a single moment abandoned the idea that many of our most vexing and painful social problems could be ameliorated if we knew how to school our young. You may conclude from this that I am a romantic, but not, I think, a fool. I know that education is not the same thing as schooling, and that, in fact, not much of our education takes place in school. Schooling may be a subversive *or* a conserving activity, but it is certainly a circumscribed one. It has a late beginning and an early end and in between it pauses for summer vacations and holidays, and generously excuses us when we are ill. To the young, schooling seems relentless, but we know it is not. What is relentless is our education, which, for good or ill, gives us no rest. That is why poverty is a great educator. Having no boundaries and refusing to be ignored, it mostly teaches hopelessness. But not always. Politics is also a great educator. Mostly it teaches, I am afraid, cynicism. But not always. Television is a great educator as well. Mostly it teaches consumerism. But not always.

It is the "not always" that keeps the romantic spirit alive in those who write about schooling. The faith is that despite some of the more debilitating teachings of culture itself, something can be done in school that will alter the lenses through which one sees the world; which is to say, that non-trivial schooling can provide a point of view from which what *is* can be seen clearly, what *was* as a living present, and what *will be* as filled with possibility.

What this means is that at its best, schooling can be about how to make a life, which is quite different from how to make a living. Such an enterprise is not easy to pursue, since our politicians rarely speak of it, our technology is indifferent to it, and our commerce despises it. Nonetheless, it is the weightiest and most important thing to write about.

Not everyone agrees, of course. In tracking what people have to say about schooling, I notice that most of the conversation is about means, rarely about ends. Should we privatize our schools? Should we have national standards of assessment? How should we use computers? What use can we make of television? How shall we teach reading? And so on. Some of these questions are interesting and some are not. But what they have in common is that they evade the issue of what schools are for. It is as if we are a nation of technicians, consumed by our expertise in how something should be done, afraid or incapable of thinking about why.

I write this book in the hope of altering, a little bit, the definition of the "school problem"—from means to ends. "End," of course, has at least two important meanings: "purpose" and "finish." Either meaning may apply to the future of schools, depending on whether or not there ensues a serious dialogue about purpose. By giving the book its ambiguous title, I mean to suggest that without a transcendent and honorable purpose schooling must reach its finish, and the sooner we are done with it, the better. With such a purpose, schooling becomes the central institution through which the young may find reasons for continuing to educate themselves.

PART I

1 · The Necessity of Gods

In considering how to conduct the schooling of our young, adults have two problems to solve. One is an engineering problem; the other, a metaphysical one. The engineering problem, as all such problems are, is essentially technical. It is the problem of the *means* by which the young will become learned. It addresses the issues of where and when things will be done, and, of course, how learning is supposed to occur. The problem is not a simple one, and any self-respecting book on schooling must offer some solutions to it.

But it is important to keep in mind that the engineering of learning is very often puffed up, assigned an importance it does not deserve. As an old saying goes, There are one and twenty ways to sing tribal lays, and all of them are correct. So it is with learning. There is no one who can say that this or that is the best way to know things, to feel things, to see things, to remember things, to apply things, to connect things and that no other will do as well. In fact, to make such a claim is to trivialize learning, to reduce it to a mechanical skill.

Of course, there are many learnings that are little else but a mechanical skill, and in such cases, there well may be a best way. But to become a different person because of something you have learned—to appropriate an insight, a concept, a vision, so that your world is altered—that is a different matter.

For that to happen, you need a reason. And this is the metaphysical problem I speak of.

A reason, as I use the word here, is different from a motivation. Within the context of schooling, motivation refers to a temporary psychic event in which curiosity is aroused and attention is focused. I do not mean to disparage it. But it must not be confused with a reason for being in a classroom, for listening to a teacher, for taking an examination, for doing homework, for putting up with school even if you are not motivated.

This kind of reason is somewhat abstract, not always present in one's consciousness, not at all easy to describe. And yet for all that, without it schooling does not work. For school to make sense, the young, their parents, and their teachers must have a god to serve, or, even better, several gods. If they have none, school is pointless. Nietzsche's famous aphorism is relevant here: "He who has a *why* to live can bear with almost any *how*." This applies as much to learning as to living.

To put it simply, there is no surer way to bring an end to schooling than for it to have no end.

By a god to serve, I do not necessarily mean *the* God, who is supposed to have created the world and whose moral injunctions as presented in sacred texts have given countless people a reason for living and, more to the point, a reason for learning. In the Western world, beginning in the thirteenth century and for five hundred years afterward, that God was sufficient justification for the founding of institutions of learning, from grammar schools, where children were taught to read the Bible, to great universities, where men were trained to be ministers of God. Even today, there are some schools in the West, and most in the Islamic world, whose central purpose is to serve and celebrate the glory of God. Wherever this is the case, there is no school problem, and certainly no school crisis. There may be some disputes over what subjects best promote piety, obedience, and faith; there may be students who are skeptical, even teachers who are nonbelievers. But at the core of such schools, there is a transcendent, spiritual idea that gives purpose and clarity to learning. Even the skeptics and nonbelievers know why they are there, what they are supposed to be learning, and why they are resistant to it. Some also know why they should leave.

A few years ago, I had a sad conversation with a brilliant and popular philosophy professor at Principia College, in Elsah, Illinois. Principia was and, as far as I know, still is, the only institution of higher learning of the Christian Science Church. He told me that his years at Principia had been the happiest he had known, but that he had taken a job at a secular university because he no longer believed in the tenets of Christian Science. The courses he taught, I should say, did not include discussions of, let alone instruction in, those tenets. No one other than himself need ever have known of his disaffection. But he no longer believed in the purpose of the institution, and every course, irrespective of its content, was infused with the spirit of a narrative he could not accept. So he left. I have always hoped that this forlorn professor eventually found another god to serve, another narrative to give meaning to his teaching.

With some reservations but mostly with conviction, I use the word *narrative* as a synonym for *god*, with a small *g*. I know it is risky to do so, not only because the word *god*, having an aura of sacredness, is not to be used lightly, but also because it calls to mind a fixed figure or image. But it is the purpose of such figures or images to direct one's mind to an idea and, more to my point, to a story—not any kind of story, but one that tells of origins and envisions a future, a story that constructs ideals, prescribes rules of conduct, provides a source of authority, and, above all, gives a sense of continuity and purpose. A god, in the sense I am using the word, is the name of a great narrative, one that has sufficient credibility, complexity, and symbolic power to enable one to organize one's life around it. I use the word in the same sense, for example, as did Arthur Koestler in calling his book about communism's deceptions and disappointments *The God That Failed.* His intention was to show that communism was not merely an experiment in government or social life, and still less an economic theory, but a comprehensive narrative about what the world is like, how things got to be the way they are, and what lies ahead. He also wished to show that for all of communism's contempt for the "irrational" narratives of traditional religions, it relied nonetheless on faith and dogma. It certainly had its own conception of blasphemy and heresy, and practiced a grotesque and brutal method of excommunication.

By giving this example, I do not mean to suggest that gods *must* fail—far from it, although, of course, there are many that do. My own life has been contemporaneous with the emergence of three catastrophic narratives: the gods of communism, fascism, and Nazism, each of which held out the promise of heaven but led only to hell. As you will see if you proceed to succeeding chapters, there are several other gods that have captured the hearts and minds of people but that, I believe, are inadequate to provide a profound reason either for living or for learning. And if you proceed even further, you will see that I believe there are life- and learning-enhancing narratives that are available if only we would give them sufficient attention: These are gods *that* serve, as well as gods *to* serve.

Nonetheless, my intention here is neither to bury nor to praise any gods, but to claim that we cannot do without them, that whatever else we may call ourselves, we are the god-making species. Our genius lies in our capacity to make meaning through the creation of narratives that give point to our labors, exalt our history, elucidate the present, and give direction to our future. To do their work, such narratives do not have to be "true" in a scientific sense. There are many enduring narratives whose details include things that are false to observable fact. The purpose of a narrative is to give meaning to the world, not to describe it scientifically. The measure of a narrative's "truth" or "falsity" is in its consequences: Does it provide people with a sense of personal identity, a sense of a community life, a basis for moral conduct, explanations of that which cannot be known?

You will recognize that this kind of storytelling goes by many different names. Joseph Campbell and Rollo May refer to it as "myth." Freud, who understood better than anyone the creative source and psychic need of such tales, nonetheless called them "illusions." One may even say, without much of a stretch, that Marx had something of this in mind in using the word *ideology*. But it is not my point to differentiate with scholarly nuance the subtle variations among these terms. The point is that, call them what you will, we are unceasing in creating histories and futures for ourselves through the medium of narrative. Without a narrative, life has no meaning. Without meaning, learning has no purpose. Without a purpose, schools are houses of detention, not attention. This is what my book is about.

The most comprehensive narratives are, of course, found in such texts as the Old Testament, the New Testament, the Koran, the Bhagavad Gita. But beginning in the sixteenth century, at least in the West, there began to emerge narratives of a different sort, although with power enough to serve as alternate gods. Among the most enduring is the great narrative known as "inductive science." It is worth noting of this god that its first storytellers—Descartes, Bacon, Galileo, Kepler, and Newton, for example—did not think of their story as a replacement for the great Judeo-Christian narrative, but as an extension of it. In fact, the point has been made more than once that the great age of science was based on a belief in a God who was himself a scientist and technician, and who would therefore approve of a civilization committed to such an enterprise. "For all we know," Eric Hoffer wrote, "one of the reasons that other civilizations, with all their ingenuity and skill, did not develop a machine age is that they lacked a God whom they could readily turn into an all-powerful engineer. For has not the mighty Jehovah performed from the beginning of time the feats that our machine age is even now aspiring to achieve?"[1] Galileo, Kepler, and Newton would largely agree, conceiving of God, as they did, as a great clockmaker and mathematician. In any case, there is no doubt that from the beginning of the age of science, its creators believed in the great narrative of Jehovah. Their discoveries were made in the service of the Judeo-Christian God. And could they know of Stephen Hawking's remark that the research permitted by the (now abandoned) supercollider would give insight into the mind of God, they would be pleased. The difference between them and Hawking is that Hawking, as an avowed atheist, does not believe what he said. To him, the story of Jehovah's wonders is only a dead metaphor, perhaps a tale told by an idiot. Apparently, the great story of science, all by itself, is enough for Hawking, as it has been for many others. It is a story that exalts human reason, places criticism over faith, disdains revelation as a source of knowledge, and, to put a spiritual cast upon it, postulates (as Jacob Bronowski has done) that our purpose on Earth is to discover reliable knowledge. Of course, the great narrative of science shares with the great religious narratives the idea that there is order to the universe, which is a fundamental assumption of all important narratives.

In fact, science even has a version (of sorts) of the concept of the "mind of God." As Bertrand Russell once put it, if there is a God, it is a differential equation. Kepler, in particular, would probably have liked that way of thinking about the matter; and perhaps that, after all, is what Stephen Hawking meant. In any case, the great strength of the science-god is, of course, that it works—far better than supplication, far better than even Francis Bacon could have imagined. Its theories are demonstrable and cumulative; its errors, correctable; its results, practical. The science-god sends people to the moon, inoculates people against disease, transports images through vast spaces so that they can be seen in our living rooms. It is a mighty god and, like more ancient ones, gives people a measure of control over their lives, which is one of the reasons why gods are invented in the first place. Some say the science-god gives more control and more power than any other god before it.

Nonetheless, like all gods, it is imperfect. Its story of our origins and of our end is, to say the least, unsatisfactory. To the question, How did it all begin?, science answers, Probably by an accident. To the question, How will it all end?, science answers, Probably by an accident. And to many people, the accidental life is not worth living. Moreover, regarding the question, What moral instruction do you give us?, the science-god maintains a tight-lipped silence. It places itself at the service of both the beneficent and the cruel, and its grand moral impartiality, if not indifference, has made it welcome the world over. More precisely, it is its offspring that is so welcomed. For like another god, the God who produced a Son and a Holy Ghost, the science-god has spawned another—the great narrative of technology. This is a wondrous and energetic story, which, with greater clarity than its father, offers us a vision of paradise. Whereas the science-god speaks to us of both understanding and power, the technology-god speaks only of power. It demolishes the assertion of the Christian God that heaven is only a posthumous reward. It offers convenience, efficiency, and prosperity here and now; and it offers its benefits to all, the rich as well as the poor, as does the Christian God. But it goes much further. For it does not merely give comfort to the poor; it promises that through devotion to it the poor will become rich. Its record of achievement—there can be no doubt—has been formidable, in part because it is a demanding god, and is strictly monotheistic. Its first commandment is a familiar one: "Thou shalt have no other gods before me." This means that those who follow its path must shape their needs and aspirations to the possibilities of technology. No other god can be permitted to impede, slow down, frustrate, or, least of all, oppose the sovereignty of technology. Why this is necessary is explained with fierce clarity in the second and third commandments. "We are the Technological Species," says the second, "and therein lies our genius." "Our destiny," says the third, "is to replace ourselves with machines, which means that technological ingenuity and human progress are one and the same."

Those who are skeptical about these propositions, who are inclined to take the name of the technology-god in vain, are condemned as reactionary renegades, especially when they speak of gods of a different kind. Among those who have risked heresy was Max Frisch, who remarked, "Technology is the knack of so arranging the world that we do not experience it."[2] But he and other such heretics have been cast aside and made to bear the damning mark of "Luddite" all of their days. There are also those, like Aldous Huxley, who believed that the great god of Technology might be sufficiently tamed so that its claims were more modest. He once said that if he had rewritten *Brave New World*, ". . . he would have included a sane alternative, a society in which 'science and technology would be used as though, like the Sabbath, they had been made for man, not (as at present and still more so in the *Brave New World*) as though man were to be adapted and enslaved to them.' "[3]

Although both my words and tone will suggest I believe with Frisch and Huxley that the technology-god is a false one (I do, of course), I will hold that point until later. Here, I wish to stress that all gods are imperfect, even dangerous. A belief too strongly held, one that excludes the possibility of a tolerance for other gods, may result in a psychopathic fanaticism. That is what Jesus meant (and Huxley in referring to it) when he said, "The sabbath was made for man, and not man for the sabbath." We may recall here a remark made by Niels Bohr that bears on this point. He said: "The opposite of a correct statement is an incorrect statement, but the opposite of a profound truth is another profound truth."[4] He meant to teach us, as have other wise people, that it is better to have access to more than one profound truth. To be able to hold comfortably in one's mind the validity and usefulness of two contradictory truths is the source of tolerance, openness, and, most important, a sense of humor, which is the greatest enemy of fanaticism. Nonetheless, it is undoubtedly better to have one profound truth, one god, one narrative, than to have none.

What happens to people when they have no gods to serve? Some commit suicide. There is more of this in the United States, particularly among our young, than in most other places in the world. Some envelop themselves in drugs, including alcohol. Some take whatever pleasure is to be found in random violence. Some encase themselves in an impenetrable egoism. Many, apparently, find a momentary and piti-ful release from dread in commercial re-creations of once-powerful narratives of the past.

I have before me an account of the proliferation of "theme parks" in both the United States and Europe. As I write, one of them is about to arise in Poland, where, according to *Travel and Leisure* magazine, its staff will dress in replica uniforms of the Luftwaffe and Wehrmacht to inspire nightly dances at "Hitler's Bunker Disco." Another, an amusement park near Berlin, will take as its theme "East Germany under Commu-nism." Its service people will pretend to be agents of the secret police, and will put those making critical remarks about the government into a fake jail. Across the ocean, near Atlanta, Georgia, an amusement park is being developed around the theme "Gone With the Wind Country." Not to be outdone, the Walt Disney Company, whose prosperity is entirely based on the timely and romantic re-creation of narratives, has drawn up plans for still another amusement park near Manassas, Virginia, with the theme "The Civil War Experience." Appar-ently, the exhibits are to include a dramatization of the expe-rience of slavery—whether for it or against is not yet clear (nor indeed, as I write, is the future of this project).[5]

Is all of this a mere rehearsal for the mass consumption of "virtual reality," as Joy Gould Boyum suspects? Are we being readied for a time when we will not require expensive theme parks to re-create the nightmare or fantasy of our choice, but can materialize either with the press of a button? Whether we are or not, what is certainly happening here is, to use Rollo May's phrase, a "cry for myth." Nightmare or fantasy, these parks allow one to inhabit a world where some powerful nar-rative once held sway, a narrative that gave people a reason for living, and in whose absence a kind of psychic trauma en-sues. Even if a narrative places one in hell, it is better to be there than to be nowhere. To be nowhere means to live in a barren culture, one that offers no vision of the past or future, no clear voice of authority, no organizing principles. In such a culture, what are schools for? What *can* they be for?

There was a time when American culture knew what schools were for because it offered fully functioning multiple narratives for its people to embrace. There was, for example, the great story of democracy, which the American artist Ben Shahn once proclaimed "the most appealing idea that the world has yet known." Alexis de Tocqueville called it "the principle of civic participation." Gunnar Myrdal encapsulated the idea in the phrase "The American Creed," which he judged to be the most explicitly articulated system of general ideals of any country in the West. The first chapter of the story opens with "In the beginning, there was a revolution." As the story unfolds, there arise sacred words such as "government of the people, by the people and for the people." Because he helped to write the story, Thomas Jefferson, the Moses of the great democracy-god, knew what schools were for—to ensure that citizens would know when and how to protect their liberty. This is a man who produced an essay that could have cost him his life, and that included the words: "We hold these truths to be self-evident; that all men are created equal; that they are endowed by their creator with certain unalienable rights; that among these are life, liberty, and the pursuit of happiness." It would not have come easily to the mind of such a man, as it does to political leaders today, that the young should be taught to read exclusively for the purpose of increasing their economic productivity. Jefferson had a more profound god to serve.

As did Emma Lazarus, whose poem celebrates another once-powerful American narrative. "Give me your tired, your poor, your huddled masses yearning to breathe free," she wrote. Where else, save the great narrative of Jesus, can one find a story that so ennobles the huddled masses? Here, America is portrayed as the great melting pot. Such a story answers many profound questions, including, What are schools for? Schools are to fashion Americans out of the wretched refuse of teeming shores. Schools are to provide the lost and lonely with a common attachment to America's history and future, to America's sacred symbols, to its promise of freedom. The schools are, in a word, the affirmative answer to the question, Can a coherent, stable, unified culture be created out of people of diverse traditions, languages, and religions?

There have been, of course, other narratives that have served to give guidance and inspiration to people, and, especially, that have helped to give purpose to schooling. Among them is one that goes by the name of the Protestant ethic. In this tale, it is claimed that hard work and a disciplined capacity to delay gratification are the surest path toward earning God's favor. Idle hands do the Devil's work, as do lustful and, often, merely pleasurable thoughts. Although this god of self-control is a legacy of the Calvinist Puritans who founded America, its power extended to many of the huddled masses who came from quite different traditions. They, of course, brought with them their own narratives, which in the context of America served—we might say—as "local gods," but gods with sufficient power to give point to schooling.

Here I can offer my own schooling as an example. I grew up learning to love the American Creed while at the same time being inspired by a more "tribal" story, to which I had (and still have) considerable attachment. As the child of Jewish parents, I was required to go to two schools: the American public school, in which the names of Washington, Jefferson, Madison, Tom Paine, and Lincoln were icons, and a "Jewish"

school, in which the names of Abraham, Sarah, Isaac, Re-
becca, Jacob, Rachel, Leah, and Moses were equally sacred. (It
should be noted that the democracy-story has almost no significant women; the chosen-people-story has plenty.) As presented to me, the democracy-story did not conflict with the
chosen-people-story; neither did the great melting-pot-story,
nor, astonishingly enough, did the Protestant-ethic-story
(perhaps because it is not much different from "Jewish guilt,"
which proceeds from the assumption that whatever happens,
it is your fault).

The point is (putting guilt aside) that the great American
narratives share with my tribal one certain near-universal
themes and principles—for example, family honor, restraint,
social responsibility, humility, and empathy for the outcast.
Integrating these narratives was not difficult for me or for my
public school classmates, who were, among others, Irish,
Greek, Italian, and German, and who had their own tribal
tales to enrich and mesh with the great narratives being
taught in school.

I might add that it did not occur to many of us that the
school was obliged to praise our tribal stories or even to discuss them. For one thing, we did not believe our teachers
were qualified to do so. For another, the teachers gave no hint
that they thought it within their province. For still another,
our classes were far too multicultural to make it a practical
goal. The schools, it seemed to us, had no business to conduct
with "ethnicity." (The term itself, incidentally, was unknown
to us at the time, since it was first used in 1940 by W. Lloyd
Warner and did not enter common usage until much later.)
The promotion of ethnicity, we believed, was the responsibility of the home, where, among other things, a "tribal" language could be spoken freely (in my case, Yiddish) and where
religious traditions and holidays were honored and "non-

American" food was consumed. The task was also taken up by one's church or synagogue, by fraternal organizations, and even to some extent by local political associations. Some of our ethnic stories were also told in the popular arts—in movies, for example. In this respect, the Irish did extraordinarily well, being depicted in many films as hardworking, family-oriented, fun-loving people whose priests sang liltingly and whose nuns were beautiful. The Jews and Italians didn't fare as well, the Greeks were ignored, the blacks were humiliated, and, of course, the Germans were savaged. Nonetheless, we did not expect the schools to make compensation. Only to make Americans.

I am aware, of course, that the situation I have just described was not entirely uniform or, I should say, satisfactory. As early as 1915, grievances were expressed against the melting-pot metaphor and more particularly against its supposed reality.[6] While it was conceded that the American Creed was based predominantly on an Anglo-Saxon tradition, the argument was made that its principles were being enacted largely by immigrants, who enriched it by their own traditions and who, in any case, would not abandon their tribal identities. Thus, the idea of cultural pluralism entered the schools, mostly beginning in the 1930s. This meant that in many public schools (not mine), the history, literature, and traditions of different immigrant groups were included as part of the great tale of the American Creed. I do not know if the self-esteem and ethnic pride of the children of the huddled masses were elevated by cultural pluralism. Probably yes in some cases; maybe no, with accompanying embarrassment, in a few. Although my own schools were considerably late in adopting cultural pluralism, I do remember an occasion when a teacher, in a rare gesture of accommodation to ethnic diversity, made a point of emphasizing the contribution of the Jew

Haim Salomon to the financing of the Revolutionary War. The financing? I would have much preferred if Salomon had been Paul Revere's backup.

Whatever the gains or losses may have been in the self-esteem of the students, cultural pluralism made three positive contributions toward maintaining the vitality and usefulness of the narratives underlying the public school experience. First, it provided a fuller and more accurate picture of American culture and, especially, its history—which is to say, it revealed the dynamic nature of the great American narratives. Melting pot or not, America was shown to be a composite culture from which, in principle, none were excluded. Second, at no point was the inclusion of the immigrant narratives presented as a refutation of the American Creed. Even the horrendous stories of the massacre of "native" Americans, slavery, and the exploitation of "coolie" labor could be told without condemning the ideals of democracy, the melting pot, or the Protestant ethic. Indeed, such stories often served as an inspiration to purify the American Creed, to overcome prejudice, to redeem ourselves from the blighted parts of our history. Third, the inclusion of any immigrant narrative was not intended to promote divisiveness among different groups. The idea was to show that there were substance and richness in each tribal tale, and that we were better for knowing the gods of other people.

It would seem that certain versions of what is now called "multiculturalism" reject all three of these ideas, and this rejection, I will soon argue, seriously threatens the future of *public*, as opposed to private, schools. Here, I will say only that the idea of public education depends absolutely on the existence of shared narratives *and* the exclusion of narratives that lead to alienation and divisiveness. What makes public schools public is not so much that the schools have common goals but that the students have common gods. The reason for this is that public education does not serve a public. It *creates* a public. And in creating the right kind of public, the schools contribute toward strengthening the spiritual basis of the American Creed. That is how Jefferson understood it, how Horace Mann understood it, how John Dewey understood it. And, in fact, there is no other way to understand it. The question is not, Does or doesn't public schooling create a public? The question is, What kind of public does it create? A conglomerate of self-indulgent consumers? Angry, soulless, directionless masses? Indifferent, confused citizens? Or a public imbued with confidence, a sense of purpose, a respect for learning, and tolerance? The answer to this question has nothing whatever to do with computers, with testing, with teacher accountability, with class size, and with the other details of managing schools. The right answer depends on two things, and two things alone: the existence of shared narratives and the capacity of such narratives to provide an inspired reason for schooling.

2 · Some Gods That Fail

It has not been a good century for gods, or even a good century and a half. Charles Darwin, we might say, began the great assault by revealing that we were not the children of God but of monkeys. His revelation took its toll on him; he suffered from unrelieved stomach and bowel pains for which medical historians have failed to uncover a physical cause. Nonetheless, Darwin was unrepentant and hoped that many people would find inspiration, solace, and continuity in the great narrative of evolution. But not many have, and the psychic trauma he induced continues barely concealed to our own day. Karl Marx, who invited Darwin to write an introduction to *Das Kapital* (Darwin declined), tore to shreds the god of Nationalism, showing, with theory and countless examples, how the working classes are deluded into identifying with their capitalist tormentors. Sigmund Freud, working quietly in his consulting room at Bergasse 19 in Vienna, bid fair to become the world's most ferocious god-buster. He showed that the great god of Reason, whose authority had been certified by the Age of Enlightenment, was a great imposter, that it served mostly to both rationalize and conceal the commands of our most primitive urgings. The cortex, as it were, is merely the servant of Genitalia. An original but soul-searing idea, it may even be true. All of this not being enough,

Freud destroyed the story of childhood innocence and, for good measure, tried to prove that Moses was not a Jew (for which he apologized but did not recant) and argued that our belief in deities was a childish and neurotic illusion. Even the gentle Albert Einstein, though not himself an Einsteinian, contributed to the general disillusionment, wreaking havoc on Isaac Newton's science-god—a Freudian instance, if ever there was one, of the son slaying the father. Einstein's revolutionary papers led to the idea that we do not see things as they are but as *we* are. The oldest axiom of survival—seeing is believing—was brought to heel. Its opposite—believing is seeing—turned out to be at least as true. Moreover, Einstein's followers have concluded, and believe they have proved, that complete knowledge is unattainable. Try as we will, we can *never* know certain things—not because we lack intelligence, not even because we are enclosed in a prison of protoplasm, but because the universe is, well, malicious.

The odd thing is that though they differed in temperament, each of these men intended to provide us with a firmer and more humane basis for our beliefs. And someday that may yet happen. Meanwhile, humanity reels from what has been lost. God is dead, Nietzsche said before he went insane. He may have meant gods are dead. If he did, he was wrong. In this century, new gods have rushed in to replace the old, but most have had no staying power (which is, perhaps, what Nietzsche was prophesying). I have already alluded to three of them: the gods of communism, Nazism, and fascism. The first claimed to represent the story of history itself, and so could be supposed to serve as an inspiration until the final triumph of the proletariat. It ended rather suddenly, shockingly, and without remorse, in a rubble of stone on the outskirts of West Berlin, leaving the proletariat to wonder if history, like the universe, is also malicious. Hitler's great tale had an even shorter run. He prophesied that the Third Reich would last a thousand years, perhaps longer than history itself. His story began with a huge bonfire whose flames were meant to consume, once and for all, the narratives of all other gods. It ended twelve years later, also in fire and also in Berlin, the body of its godhead mutilated beyond recognition.

Of fascism we may say it has not yet had its final hour. It lingers here and there, though hardly as a story worth telling. Where it still exists, people do not *believe* in it, they endure it. And so, Francis Fukuyama tells us in *The End of History*, the great narrative of liberal democracy has triumphed at last and brings an end to history's dialectic. Which is why so many people look to America with anxious eyes to see if its gods may serve them as well.

So far, America's answer has largely been, Believe in a market economy, which is not much of a story, not much of an answer. The problem is that America's better gods have been badly wounded. As America has moved toward the status of an empire (known today, with moral ambiguity, maybe even irony, as the world's only "superpower"), its great story of liberal democracy has lost much of its luster. Of Tocqueville's "civic participation," there is less in America than in any other industrialized nation. Half of America's eligible voters do not take the trouble to go to the polls in presidential elections, and many who do form their opinions by watching, leaden-eyed, television campaign commercials. It would be frightening to contemplate how few know the names of their representatives in Congress, or who is the secretary of state, or how many even know that there *is* such a cabinet post. Some of this civic indifference is doubtless connected to the cynicism generated by the crude fabrications of recent American leaders, especially Lyndon Johnson and Richard Nixon, the latter of whom made the term *cover-up* commonplace in political discourse. Moreover, the idea that America, through an enlightened foreign policy, may serve as a moral light unto nations was dimmed, to say the least, in the jungles of Vietnam, and then made ridiculous in Granada, Panama, and Kuwait. Could Marx have had something like this in mind when he said that history repeats itself, first as tragedy and then as farce?

I do not say the idea of America as a moral metaphor is dead. Were it dead, the students in Tienanmen Square would not have used the Statue of Liberty as their symbol; the students in Prague would not have surged through the streets reading aloud from the works of Thomas Jefferson; and armies of immigrants would not be landing each day at John F. Kennedy Airport yearning to breathe free. Through all the turmoil, it is well to keep in mind that a wounded god is different from a dead one. We may yet have need of this one.

Meanwhile, the narrative of the great melting-pot has also suffered as many insults as an imperfect god can bear. For some, for example, Koreans, Chinese, and Russians, it has worked tolerably well, but too many others have been blocked from sharing in the fullness of the American promise because of their race or native language. The case of African-Americans in particular is a grotesque contradiction of the romance of a blended society, all the more so because they are not immigrants at all, but as native as most Americans get. Although there has been an astonishing growth of a black middle class, which is supposed to be the test of a group's acceptance into the mainstream, for millions of blacks the American dream is a nightmare of poverty, family disintegration, violence, and joblessness. These matters were supposed to have been addressed by a forty-year commitment to social equality, which included such amendments to the melting-pot-story as school integration, the Civil Rights Act, open admission policies, and affirmative action. And yet for all of that, blacks remain, as Ralph Ellison would say it, invisible people. On the day I am writing this, for example, Americans have been cheered by some news issued by the Bureau of Labor Statistics: Unemployment is down, indicating the economy is on the rise and better times are ahead. Barely commented upon and of almost no interest is the fact that black unemployment has increased, as has (other figures show) black homelessness, especially among children. It is as if America wishes to proceed with its business without the inclusion of blacks. And yet, it is one of the truly remarkable (and largely ignored) facts of American culture that millions of blacks continue to believe in America's promises and in its great narratives, perhaps more deeply than do any others.

There are, of course, other groups—Latinos, for example— who seem unable to find a welcoming place for themselves in the melting pot and who therefore find something less than inspiration in the promise embedded in its story. As for the rigorous tale of the blessedness of Hard Work, too many Americans no longer believe in it. The great school of the Higher Learning, television, teaches them that a dream deferred is a dream forever denied—which is to say, no dream at all; that they are, in fact, entitled to the fruits of technology's largesse; and that the god of Consumership confers its graciousness more freely than can any god of Labor.

I will come to the promise of the god of Consumership in a few pages. Here it needs only to be said that in America, as elsewhere, there exists what Vaclav Havel calls "a crisis in narrative." Old gods have fallen, either wounded or dead. New ones have been aborted. "We are looking," he said, "for new scientific recipes, new ideologies, new control systems, new institutions. . . ." In other words, we seek new gods who can provide us with "an elementary sense of justice, the ability to see things as others do, a sense of transcendental responsibility, archetypal wisdom, good taste, courage, compassion, and faith."[1]

Havel does not underestimate the difficulties in this. He knows that skepticism, disillusionment, alienation—and all the other words we use to describe a loss of meaning—have come to characterize our age, affecting every social institution, not least the schools. Having once been president of Czechoslovakia, and having lost the Slovaks to their own gods, Havel knows, better than anyone, that the almost worldwide return to "tribalism" signifies a search to recover a source of transcendent identity and values. He also knows, as many others do, how dangerous such searches can be, which is why no one need be surprised by the rise in the West of skinheads, who have revived the symbols and programs of Nazism, or, as I write, the emerging popularity in Russia of Vladimir Zhirinovsky, the "Russian Hitler," who promises the masses a future more fully articulated than a conversion to a market economy. Zhirinovsky takes his story from hell, but we must grant him this: He knows as well as Havel that people need gods as much as food.

Neither should we be surprised that there has arisen, especially though not exclusively in American academic circles, a kind of metaphysics of meaninglessness, known popularly as the philosophy of "deconstruction." Invented, so to say, by a reformed Nazi sympathizer, Paul de Man, deconstruction postulates that the meanings of words are always indeterminate, that words are less about reality than about other words, and that the search for definite meaning in words or anyplace else is pointless, since there is nothing to find. How he came to this conclusion is not entirely clear—perhaps he wished us to believe, by way of self-justification, that it is possible to read *Mein Kampf* as a paean of praise to the Jewish race.

In any case, no philosophy of deconstruction can conceal the crisis in narrative, the decline of once-sturdy gods. The carnage is painfully visible, for example, in the trivial uses to which sacred symbols are now put, especially in the United States. There can, of course, be no functioning sense of a great narrative without a measure of respect for its symbols. How are such symbols now used? Take almost any of America's once great narratives and we can see. There is, for example, the story of our origins, summarized so eloquently in Abraham Lincoln's Gettysburg Address. It tells of a nation "brought forth" through revolution, destined to serve as an example to the rest of the world. This is the same Abraham Lincoln whose face is used to announce linen sales in February. Emma Lazarus's poem celebrating an immigrant culture is lodged at the base of the Statue of Liberty. This is the same Statue of Liberty used by an airline to persuade potential customers to fly to Miami. There is the story of a God-fearing nation seeking guidance and strength from the lessons of the Old Testament and the commandments brought by Moses. This is the same Moses who is depicted in a poster selling kosher chickens. Of Christmas and the uses made of its significant symbols, the less said the better. But it probably should be noted that Hebrew National uses both Uncle Sam and God (with a capital G) to sell frankfurters, Martin Luther King, Jr.'s birthday is largely used as an occasion for furniture sales, and the infant Jesus and Mary have been invoked to promote VH-1, a rock-music television station.

It is difficult to say if this erosion of symbols, this obliteration of the difference between the sacred and the profane, is the effect or the cause of a crisis in narrative. Mostly, I would say, the effect (although effects quickly become causes in these matters). Whichever the case, we are led to conclude that it is not a good time for gods and their symbols, and is therefore a bad time for social institutions that draw their power from metaphysical sources. This leads us at last to the question, What does all this mean for the enterprise of schooling?

The answer that comes most readily and nastily to mind is that the majority of educators have ignored the question altogether. Many have focused their attention on the engineering of learning, their journals being filled with accounts of research that show this way or that to be better for teaching reading, mathematics, or social studies. The evidence for the superiority of one method over another is usually given in the language of statistics, which, in spite of its abstract nature, is strangely referred to as "hard evidence." This gives the profession a sense of making progress, and sometimes delusions of grandeur. I recently read an article in *The American Educator* in which the author claims that teaching methods based on research in cognitive science are "the educational equivalents of polio vaccine and penicillin."[2]

From what diseases cognitive science will protect our students is not entirely clear. But in fact, it does not matter. The educational landscape is flooded with similar claims of the miracles that will flow from computer science, school choice, teacher accountability, national standards of student assessment, and whole-language learning. Why not cognitive science, as well?

There was a time when educators became famous for providing reasons for learning; now they become famous for inventing a method.

There are, of course, many things wrong with all of this, not least that it diverts attention from important matters—for example, the fundamental simplicity of teaching and learning when both teacher and student share a reason for the enterprise. As Theodore Roszak has written: "Too much apparatus, like too much bureaucracy, only inhibits the natural flow [of teaching and learning]. Free human dialogue, wandering wherever the agility of the mind allows, lies at the heart of education. If teachers do not have the time, the incentive, or the wit to provide that; if students are too demoralized, bored or distracted to muster the attention their teachers need of them, then *that* is the educational problem which has to be solved—and solved from inside the experience of the teachers and the students."[3]

That problem, as I have been saying, is metaphysical in nature, not technical. And it is sad that so many of our best minds in education do not acknowledge this. But, of course, some do, and it is neither fair nor accurate to say that educators have been entirely indifferent to the metaphysics of schooling. The truth is that school cannot exist without *some* reason for its being, and in fact there are several gods our students are presently asked to serve. It will take the rest of this chapter and all of the next for me to describe them and to show why each is incapable of sustaining, with richness, seriousness, and durability, the idea of a public school.

As it happens, the first narrative consists of such an uninspiring set of assumptions that it is hardly noticed as a narrative at all. But we may count it as one, largely because so many believe it to be the preeminent reason for schooling. It may properly go by the name of the god of Economic Utility. As its name suggests, it is a passionless god, cold and severe. But it makes a promise, and not a trivial one. Addressing the young, it offers a covenant of sorts with them: If you will pay attention in school, and do your homework, and score well on tests, and behave yourself, you will be rewarded with a well-paying job when you are done. Its driving idea is that the purpose of schooling is to prepare children for competent entry into the economic life of a community. It follows from this that any school activity not designed to further this end is seen as a frill or an ornament—which is to say, a waste of valuable time.

The origins of this worldview are traceable to several traditions, beginning, obviously, with the never-ending struggle to provide ourselves with material sustenance. People need to eat. Nothing could be plainer than that. What are schools for—what is *anything* for—if not to provide us with the means to earn our bread? But there is more to it than this. The god of Economic Utility is not entirely without a spiritual glow, dim as that might be. It does, in fact, tell a story of sorts, parts of which can be found in Adam Smith's *The Wealth of Nations*, in the tale of the Protestant ethic, and even in the writings of Karl Marx. The story tells us that we are first and foremost economic creatures, and that our sense of worth and purpose is to be found in our capacity to secure material benefits. This is one reason why the schooling of women, until recently, was not considered of high value. According to this god, you *are* what you do for a living—a rather problematic conception of human nature even if one could be assured of a stimulating and bountiful job. Nonetheless, that assurance is given through a clear delineation of good and evil. Goodness inheres in productivity, efficiency, and organization; evil in inefficiency and sloth. Like any self-respecting god, this one withholds its favor from those who are evil and bestows it abundantly on those who are good.

The story goes on to preach that America is not so much a culture as it is an economy, and that the vitality of any nation's economy rests on high standards of achievement and rigorous discipline in schools. There is little evidence (that is to say, none) that the productivity of a nation's economy is related to the quality of its schooling.[4] But every god has unsubstantiated axioms, and most people are content to let this one go unexamined. Those who believe in it are inclined to compare the achievements of American schoolchildren with those of children from other countries. The idea is to show that the Americans do not do as well in certain key subjects, thus accounting for failures in American productivity. There are several problems with this logic, among them the difficulties in comparing groups that differ greatly in their traditions, language, values, and general orientation to the world. Another is that even if it can be shown that American students are inferior in some respects—let us say in mathematics and reading—to students in certain other countries, those countries do not uniformly have higher standards of economic productivity than America. Since 1970, the U.S. economy has generated 41 million new jobs. By contrast, the entire European Union, whose population is close to one-third larger than that of the United States, has created only 8 million new jobs. And all this has occurred during a period when American students have performed less well than European students.[5] Moreover, it can be rather easily shown from an historical perspective that during periods of high economic productivity in America, levels of educational achievement were not especially high.

The whole business is, to say the least, problematic, and most industrial nations give no credence to it. That is why, for example, the Germans and Japanese are opening huge automobile plants in America, and in states not famous for the excellence of their educational systems. Even if one argued that such investments are made because labor is cheaper in America, companies like Mercedes-Benz, BMW, and Honda would surely not proceed with billion-dollar investments if they believed the inferior education of Americans prevented them from producing automobiles of competitive quality.

One need hardly add that the story of the god of Economic

Utility is rarely believed by students and certainly has almost no power to inspire them. Generally, young people have too much curiosity about the world and far too much vitality to be attracted to an idea that reduces them to a single dimension. I did know a youngster once—he was in the second grade—who, upon being asked what he wanted to be when he grew up, answered without hesitation, "An orthodontist." It is hard to imagine a more depressing answer. It is unnatural for children to regard themselves as economic units except under extreme circumstances, and probably not even then. Nonetheless, since his parents had clearly put that idea into his head, I assume they would have approved. Many parents, in fact, are apt to like the idea of school as a primary training ground for future employment, as do many corporate executives. This is why the story of Economic Utility is told and re-told in television commercials and political speeches as the reason why children should go to school, and stay in school, and why schools should receive public support.

But for all its widespread popularity, the god of Economic Utility is impotent to create satisfactory reasons for schooling. Putting aside its assumption that education and productivity go hand in hand, its promise of providing interesting employment is, like the rest of it, overdrawn. There is no strong evidence for believing that well-paying, stimulating jobs will be available to most students upon graduation. Since 1980, in America at least, the largest increase in jobs has been for those with relatively low skills—for example, waiters, porters, salespeople, taxi drivers. I mean no disrespect to those who do these jobs competently, but their skills are hardly so complex that the schools must be preoccupied with teaching them. In fact, almost anything the schools might teach would be suitable for preparing the young for such work. Of course, well-paying, highly competitive jobs will be available, as always, to those with a high degree of competence in the uses of language. But no serious argument can be made, not even by orthodontists, that the sole reason why language competence is useful is to ensure entry into a privileged profession. Even if such a proposition were put forward, we would not know which professions our students might aspire to, and therefore we would not know what specialized competence they would require. If we knew, for example, that all our students wished to be corporate executives, would we train them to be good readers of memos, quarterly reports, and stock quotations, and not bother their heads with poetry, science, history? I think not. Everyone who thinks, thinks not. Specialized competence can come only through a more generalized competence, which is to say that economic utility is a by-product of a good education. Any education that is mainly *about* economic utility is far too limited to be useful, and, in any case, so diminishes the world that it mocks one's humanity. At the very least, it diminishes the idea of what a good learner is.

Sad to say, some of America's most important political leaders believe that one who learns how to be useful economically will have learned how to be an educated person. A headline, early in 1994, announced: CLINTON TELLS EDUCATORS YOUTHS ARE NOT GETTING PRACTICAL SKILLS FOR JOBS.[6] The story quotes the President as saying, "In the nineteenth century, at most, young Americans needed a high school education to make their way. . . . It was good enough if they could read well and understand basic numbers. In the twenty-first century, our people will have to keep learning all their lives." Of course, in the nineteenth century it was also desirable for people to continue learning all their lives. In fact, there was far more technological change in the nineteenth century than is likely to occur in the twenty-first. The nineteenth century gave us telegraphy, photography, the rotary press, the telephone, the typewriter, the phonograph, the transatlantic cable, the electric light, movies, the locomotive, rockets, the steamboat, the X ray, the revolver, the computer, and the stethoscope, not to mention canned food, the penny press, the modern magazine, the advertising agency, the modern bureaucracy, and, for God's sake, even the safety pin. But let us suppose the President did not learn about this in Arkansas schools and was advancing the standard-brand argument that with continuing, rapid technological change the job market will require people who are adaptable to change, who can learn new concepts easily, and who can discard unusable assumptions without trauma. This is a very difficult task for the schools, and one that John Dewey held to be of the utmost importance. The President's solution is to provide the young with more practical vocational skills, which appears to be, not surprisingly, the same solution offered to California educators by Labor Secretary Robert Reich and Education Secretary Richard Riley.[7] Of course, this is exactly the wrong solution, since the making of adaptable, curious, open, questioning people has nothing to do with vocational training and everything to do with humanistic and scientific studies. The President's speech and the advice of his colleagues demonstrate that they themselves have difficulty discarding outmoded assumptions, including their belief that if something is not working—for example, training people for jobs—then what is needed is more of it.

Yet it must be admitted that the President and all his men were cheered, and cheered by educators, for placing the god of Economic Utility before all others. One may well wonder, then, why this god has so much strength, why the preparation for making a living, *which is well served by any decent edu-*

cation, should be assigned a metaphysical position of such high station. I believe the reason is that the god of Economic Utility is coupled with another god, one with a smiling face and one that provides an answer to the question, If I get a good job, then what?

I refer here to the god of Consumership, whose basic moral axiom is expressed in the slogan "Whoever dies with the most toys, wins"—that is to say, goodness inheres in those who buy things; evil in those who do not. The similarity between this god and the god of Economic Utility is obvious, but with this difference: The latter postulates that you *are* what you do for a living; the former that you *are* what you accumulate.

Devotion to the god of Consumership serves easily as the metaphysical basis of schooling because it is urged on the young early in their lives, long before they get to school—in fact, as soon as they are exposed to the powerful teachings of the advertising industry. In America, for example, the preeminent advertising medium is television, and television viewing usually begins at age eighteen months, getting serious by age three. This is the age at which children begin to ask for products they see advertised on television and sing the jingles accompanying them. Between the ages of three and eighteen, the average American youngster will see about 500,000 television commercials, which means that the television commercial is the single most substantial source of values to which the young are exposed. On the face of it, the proposition that life is made worthwhile by buying things would not seem to be an especially engrossing message, but two things make it otherwise. The first is that the god of Consumership is intimately connected with still another great narrative, the god of Technology. The second is that the television messages sent about consumership and technology come largely in the form of religious parables. This second point is not discussed as much as it ought to be, and I pause here to speak of it to emphasize the fact that the god of Consumership has a theology that cannot be taken lightly.

Of course, not every commercial has religious content. Just as in church the pastor will sometimes call the congregation's attention to nonecclesiastical matters, so there are television commercials that are entirely secular. Someone has something to sell; you are told what it is, where it can be obtained, and what it costs. Though these ads may be shrill and offensive, no doctrine is advanced and no theology invoked. But the majority of important television commercials take the form of religious parables organized around a coherent theology. Like all religious parables, these commercials put forward a concept of sin, intimations of the way to redemption, and a vision of Heaven. This will be obvious to those who have taken to heart the Parable of the Person with Rotten Breath, the Parable of the Stupid Investor, the Parable of the Lost Traveler's Checks, the Parable of the Man Who Runs Through Airports, or most of the hundreds of others that are part of our youth's religious education. In these parables, the root cause of evil is technological innocence, a failure to know the particulars of the beneficent accomplishments of industrial progress. This is the primary source of unhappiness, humiliation, and discord in life. Technological innocence refers not only to ignorance of detergents, drugs, sanitary napkins, cars, salves, and foodstuffs but also to ignorance of technical mechanisms such as banks and transportation systems. In a typical parable, you (that is, the surrogate "you") may come upon your neighbors while on vacation (always a sign of danger in television commercials) and discover that they have invested their money in a certain bank of whose special high interest rates you have been unaware. This is, of course, a moral disaster, as becomes clear when you learn that your neighbors' vacation will last for three weeks; yours must last only one.

The path to redemption requires that one believe the advice given in the commercial and then act upon it. Those who do both, as shown in the parable, will have found their way to Heaven, more or less in a state of ecstasy. It is probably unnecessary to say that all traditional religions reject the god of Consumership, claiming that devotion to it is a false spirituality, if not outright blasphemy. One would think that our schools would also be in explicit opposition to such a god, since education is supposed to free the young from the bondage of crude materialism. But, in fact, many of our schools, especially in recent times, have allied themselves with this god in a most emphatic way. I refer, for example, to the fact that approximately ten thousand schools have accepted the offer made by Christopher Whittle to include, daily, two minutes of commercial messages in the curriculum—the first time, to my knowledge, that an advertiser has employed the power of the state to force anyone to watch commercials. In exchange for this opportunity, Whittle offers his own ten-minute version of the news of the day and free, expensive television equipment, including a satellite dish.

That schools would accept such an arrangement reveals two things simultaneously. The first, of course, is that there is widespread support for the god of Consumership. That is to say, the schools see no contradiction between anything they might wish the students to learn and what commercials wish them to learn. The second is that there is equally wide support for the god of Technology, to which I will turn in the following chapter. Here, it is necessary to say that no reasonable argument can be made against educating the young to be consumers or to think about the kinds of employment that might interest them. But when these are elevated to the status of a metaphysical imperative, we are being told that we have reached the end of our wits—even worse, the limit of our wisdom.

3 · Some New Gods That Fail

I f one has a trusting relationship with one's students (let us say graduate students) and the subject under discussion is the same as the subject of this book, it is not altogether gauche to ask them if they believe in God (with a capital G). I have done this three or four times, and most students say they do. Their answer is preliminary to the next question: If someone you love were desperately ill and you had to choose between praying to God for his or her recovery or administering an antibiotic (as prescribed by a competent physician), which would you choose?

Most say the question is silly, since the alternatives are not mutually exclusive. Of course. But suppose they were; which would you choose? God helps those who help themselves, some say in choosing the antibiotic, and thereby getting the best of two possible belief systems. But if pushed to the wall (for example, God does not always help those who help themselves; God helps those who pray and who believe), most say the antibiotic, after noting that the question is asinine and proves nothing. Of course, the question was not asked, in the first place, to prove anything, but to begin a discussion of the nature of belief. And I do not fail to inform the students, by the way, that there has recently emerged at least some (though not conclusive) evidence of a scientific nature that when sick people are prayed for, they do better than those who aren't.[1]

As the discussion proceeds, important distinctions are made among the different meanings of "belief," but at some point it becomes far from asinine to speak of the god of Technology—in the sense that people believe technology works, that they rely on it, that it makes promises, that they are bereft when denied access to it, that they are delighted when they are in its presence, that for most people it works in mysterious ways, that they condemn people who speak against it, that they stand in awe of it, and that, in the born-again mode, they will alter their lifestyles, their schedules, their habits, and their relationships to accommodate it. If this be not a form of religious belief, what is?

In all strands of American cultural life, one can find so many examples of technological adoration that it is possible to write a book about it. And I would if it had not already been done so well. But nowhere do you find more enthusiasm for the god of Technology than among educators. In fact, there are those, like Lewis Perelman, who argue (for example, in his book *School's Out*) that modern information technologies have rendered schools entirely irrelevant, since there is now much more information available outside the classroom than inside. This is by no means considered an outlandish idea. Dr. Diane Ravitch, former Assistant U.S. Secretary of Education, envisions, with considerable relish, the challenge that technology presents to the tradition that "children (and adults) should be educated in a specific place, for a certain number of hours, and a certain number of days during the week and year." In other words, that children should be educated in school. Imagining the possibilities of an information superhighway offering perhaps a thousand channels, Dr. Ravitch assures us that:

In this new world of pedagogical plenty, children and adults will be able to dial up a program on their home television to learn whatever they want to know, at their own convenience. If Little Eva cannot sleep, she can learn algebra instead. At her home-learning station, she will tune in to a series of interesting problems that are presented in an interactive medium, much like video games. . . . Young John may decide that he wants to learn the history of modern Japan, which he can do by dialing up the greatest authorities and teachers on the subject, who will not only use dazzling graphs and illustrations, but will narrate a historical video that excites his curiosity and imagination.[2]

In this vision, there is, it seems to me, a confident and typical sense of unreality. Little Eva can't sleep, so she decides to learn a little algebra? Where did Little Eva come from, Mars? If not, it is more likely she will tune into a good movie. Young John decides that he wants to learn the history of modern Japan? How did young John come to this point? How is it that he never visited a library up to now? Or is it that he, too, couldn't sleep and decided a little modern Japanese history was just what he needed?

What Ravitch is talking about here is not a new technology but a new species of child, one that, in any case, hasn't been seen very much up to now. Of course, new technologies do make new kinds of people, which leads to a second objection to Ravitch's conception of the future. There is a kind of forthright determinism about the imagined world described in it. The technology is here or will be; we must use it because it is there; we will become the kind of people the technology requires us to be; and, whether we like it or not, we will remake our institutions to accommodate the technology. All of this must happen because it is good for us, but in any case, we have no choice.

This point of view is present in very nearly every statement about the future relation of learning to technology. And, as in Ravitch's scenario, there is always a cheery, gee-whiz tone to the prophecies. Here is one produced by the National Academy of Sciences, written by Hugh McIntosh.

> School for children of the Information Age will be vastly different than it was for Mom and Dad.
>
> Interested in biology? Design your own life forms with computer simulation.
>
> Having trouble with a science project? Teleconference about it with a research scientist.
>
> Bored with the real world? Go into a virtual physics lab and rewrite the laws of gravity.
>
> These are the kinds of hands-on learning experiences schools could be providing right now. The technologies that make them possible are already here, and today's youngsters, regardless of economic status, know how to use them. They spend hours with them every week— not in the classroom, but in their own homes and in video game centers at every shopping mall.[3]

It is always interesting to attend to the examples of learning, and the motivations that ignite them, in the songs of love that technophiles perform for us. It is, for example, not easy to imagine research scientists all over the world teleconferencing with thousands of students who are having difficulty with their science projects. I can't help thinking that most research scientists would put a stop to this rather quickly. But I find it especially revealing that in the preceding scenario, we have an example of a technological solution to a psychological problem that would seem to be exceedingly serious. We are presented with a student who is "bored with the real world." What does it mean to say someone is bored with the real world, especially one so young? Can a journey into virtual reality cure such a problem? And if it can, will our troubled youngster want to return to the real world? Confronted with a student who is bored with the real world, I don't think we can get away so easily by making available a virtual-reality physics lab.

The role that new technology should play in schools or anywhere else is something that needs to be discussed without the hyperactive fantasies of cheerleaders. In particular, the computer and its associated technologies are awesome additions to a culture, and they are quite capable of altering the psychic, let alone the sleeping, habits of our young. But like all important technologies of the past, they are Faustian bargains, giving and taking away, sometimes in equal measure, sometimes more in one way than the other. It is strange—indeed, shocking—that with the twenty-first century so close on our heels, we can still talk of new technologies as if they were unmixed blessings, gifts, as it were, from the gods. Don't we all know what the combustion engine has done for us and against us? What television is doing for us and against us? At the very least, what we need to discuss about Little Eva, Young John, and McIntosh's trio is what they will lose, and what we will lose, if they enter a world in which computer technology is their chief source of motivation, authority, and, apparently, psychological sustenance. Will they become, as Joseph Weizenbaum warns, more impressed by calculation than human judgment? Will speed of response become, more than ever, a defining quality of intelligence? If, indeed, the idea of a school will be dramatically altered, what kinds of learning will be neglected, perhaps made impossible? Is virtual reality a new form of therapy? If it is, what are its dangers?

These are serious matters, and they need to be discussed by those who actually know something about children from the planet Earth, and whose vision of children's needs, and the needs of a society, go beyond thinking of school mainly as a place for the convenient distribution of information. Schools are not now and have never been chiefly about getting information to children. That has been on the schools' agenda, of course, but it has always been way down on the list. In a moment, I will mention a few school functions that are higher, but here it needs saying that for technological utopians, the computer vaults information access to the top. This reshuffling of priorities comes, one might say, at a most inopportune time. The problem of giving people greater access to more information, faster, more conveniently, and in more diverse forms was the main technological thrust of the nineteenth century. Some folks haven't noticed it, but that problem was largely solved, so that for almost one hundred years, there has been more information available to the young outside the school than inside. That fact did not make the schools obsolete, and it does not make them obsolete now. Yes, it is true that Little Eva, the insomniac from Mars, could turn on an algebra lesson, thanks to the computer, in the wee hours of the morning. She could also, if she wished, read a book or magazine, watch television, pop a video into the VCR, turn on the radio, or listen to music. All of this she could have done before the computer. The computer does not solve any problem she has but exacerbates one. For Little Eva's problem is not how to get access to a well-structured algebra lesson, but what to do with all the information available to her during the day, as well as during sleepless nights. Perhaps this is why she couldn't sleep in the first place. Little Eva, like the rest of us, is overwhelmed by information. She lives in a culture which has 260,000 billboards, 17,000 newspapers, 12,000 periodicals, 27,000 video outlets for renting tapes, 400 million television sets, and well over 500 million radios, not including those in automobiles. There are 40,000 new book titles published every year, and each day 41 million photographs are taken. And, thanks to the computer, over 60 billion pieces of advertising junk mail arrive in our mailboxes every year. Everything from telegraphy and photography in the nineteenth century to the silicon chip in the twentieth has amplified the din of information intruding on Little Eva's consciousness. From millions of sources all over the globe, through every possible channel and medium—light waves, airwaves, ticker tapes, computer banks, telephone wires, television cables, satellites, and printing presses—information pours in. Behind it in every imaginable form of storage—on paper, on video, on audiotape, on discs, film, and silicon chips—is an even greater volume of information waiting to be retrieved. In the face of this, we might ask, What can schools do for Little Eva besides making still more information available? If there is nothing, then new technologies will indeed make schools obsolete. But in fact, there is plenty.

One thing that comes to mind, of which something will be said later in the book, is to provide her with a serious form of technology education, something quite different from instruction in using computers to process information, which, it strikes me, is a trivial thing to do, for two reasons. In the first place, approximately 35 million people have already learned how to use computers without the benefit of school instruction. If the schools do nothing, most of the population will know how to use computers in the next ten years, just as most of the population learned how to drive cars without school instruction. In the second place, what we needed to know about cars—as we need to know about computers, television, and other important technologies—is not how to use them but how *they* use us. In the case of cars, what we needed to think about in the early twentieth century was not how to drive them but what they would do to our air, our landscape, our social relations, our family life, and our cities. Suppose that in 1946, we had started to address similar questions about television: What would be its effects on our political institutions, our psychic habits, our children, our religious conceptions, our economy? Wouldn't we be better positioned today to control television's massive assault on American culture?

I am talking here about making technology itself an object of inquiry, so that Little Eva and Young John in using technologies will not be used or abused by them, so that Little Eva and Young John become more interested in asking questions about the computer than in getting answers from it.

I am not arguing against using computers in school. I am arguing against our sleepwalking attitudes toward it, against allowing it to distract us from more important things, against making a god of it. This is what Theodore Roszak warned against in *The Cult of Information:* "Like all cults," he wrote, "this one has the intention of enlisting mindless allegiance and acquiescence. People who have no clear idea of what they mean by information, or why they should want so much of it, are nonetheless prepared to believe that we live in an Information Age, which makes every computer around us what the relics of the True Cross were in the Age of Faith: emblems of salvation."[4] To this, I would add the sage observation of Alan Kay of Apple Computer. Kay is widely associated with the invention of the personal computer, and certainly has an interest in the use of computers in schools. Nonetheless, he has repeatedly said that any problems the schools cannot solve without computers, they cannot solve with them. What are some of those problems? There is, for example, the traditional task of teaching children how to behave in groups. You cannot have a democratic—indeed, civilized—community life unless people have learned how to participate in a disciplined way as part of a group. One might even say that schools have never been essentially about individualized learning. It is true, of course, that groups do not learn; individuals do. But the idea of a school is that individuals must learn in a setting in which individual needs are subordinated to group interests. Unlike other media of mass communication, which celebrate individual response and are experienced in private, the classroom is intended to tame the ego, to connect the individual with others, to demonstrate the value and necessity of group cohesion. At present, most scenarios describing the uses of computers have children solving problems alone. Little Eva, Young John, and the others are doing just that, and, in fact, they do not need the presence of other children. The presence of others may, indeed, be an annoyance. (Not all computer visionaries, I must say, take lightly the importance of a child's learning to subordinate the self. Seymour Papert's *The Children's Machine* is an imaginative example of how computers have been used to promote social cohesion, although, as I have had occasion to say to him, the same effects can be achieved without computers. Naturally, he disagrees.)

Nonetheless, like the printing press before it, the computer has a powerful bias toward amplifying personal autonomy and individual problem-solving. That is why, Papert to the contrary, most of the examples we are given picture children working alone. That is also why educators must guard against computer technology's undermining some of the important reasons for having the young assemble in school, where social cohesion and responsibility are of preeminent importance.

Although Ravitch is not exactly against what she calls "state run schools," she imagines them as something of a relic of a pre-technological age. She believes that the new technologies will offer all children equal access to information. Conjuring up a hypothetical Little Mary who is presumably from a poorer home than Little Eva, Ravitch imagines that Mary will have the same opportunities as Eva "to learn any subject, and to learn it from the same master teachers as children in the richest neighborhood."[5] For all its liberalizing spirit, this scenario contains some omissions that need to be kept in mind. One is that though new technologies may be a solution to the learning of "subjects," they work against the learning of what are called "social values," including an understanding of democratic processes. If one reads the first chapter of Robert Fulghum's *All I Ever Really Needed to Know I Learned in Kindergarten*, one will find an elegant summary of a few things Ravitch's scenario has left out. They include learning the following lessons: share everything, play fair, don't hit people, put things back where you found them, clean up your own mess, wash your hands before you eat, and, of course, flush.[6] The only thing wrong with Fulghum's idea is that no one actually has learned all these things at kindergarten's end. We have ample evidence that it takes many years of teaching these values in school before they are accepted and internalized. That is why it won't do for children to learn in isolation. The point is to place them in a setting that emphasizes collaboration, as well as sensitivity to and responsibility for others. That is also why schools require children to be in a certain place at a certain time and to follow certain rules, such as raising their hands when they wish to speak, not talking when others are talking, not chewing gum, not leaving until the bell rings, and exhibiting patience toward slower learners. This process is called making civilized people. The god of Technology does not appear interested in this function of schools. At least, it does not come up much when technology's virtues are enumerated.

The god of Technology may also have a trick or two up its sleeve about something else. It is often asserted that new technologies will equalize learning opportunities for the rich and poor. It is devoutly to be wished, but I doubt it. In the first place, it is generally understood by those who have studied the history of technology that technological change always produces winners and losers—which is to say, the benefits of new technologies are not distributed equally among the population. There are many reasons for this, among them economic differences. Even in the case of the automobile, which is a commodity most people can buy (though not all), there are wide differences between rich and poor in the quality of what is available to them. It would be quite astonishing if computer technology equalized all learning opportunities, irrespective of economic differences. One may be delighted that Little Eva's parents could afford the technology and software to make it possible for her to learn algebra at midnight. But Little Mary's parents may not be able to, may not even know such things are available. And if we say that the school could make the technology available to Little Mary (at least during the day), there may be something else Little Mary is lacking—two parents, for instance. I have before me an account of a 1994 Carnegie Corporation Report, produced by the National Center for Children in Poverty. It states that in

1960, only 5 percent of our children were born to unmarried mothers. In 1990, the figure was 28 percent. In 1960, 7 percent of our children under three lived with one parent. In 1990, 27 percent. In 1960, less than 1 percent of our children under eighteen experienced the divorce of their parents. In 1990, the figure was almost 50 percent.[7]

It turns out that Little Mary may be having sleepless nights as often as Little Eva, but not because she wants to get a leg up on algebra lessons. Maybe it is because she doesn't know who her father is, or, if she does, where he is. Maybe we now can understand why McIntosh's lad is bored with the real world. Or is he confused about it? Or terrified? Are there educators who seriously believe that these problems can be addressed by new technologies?

I do not say, of course, that schools can solve the problems of poverty, alienation, and family disintegration. But schools can *respond* to them. And they can do this because there are people in them, because these people are concerned with more than algebra lessons or modern Japanese history, and because these people can identify not only one's level of competence in algebra but one's level of rage and confusion and depression. I am talking here about children as they really come to us, not children who are invented to show us how computers may enrich their lives. Of course, I suppose it is possible that there are children who, waking at night, want to study algebra or who are so interested in their world that they yearn to know about Japan. If there be such children, and one hopes there are, they do not require expensive computers to satisfy their hunger for learning. They are on their way, with or without computers—unless, of course, they do not care about others, or have no friends, or little respect for democracy, or are filled with suspicion about those who are not like them. When we have machines that know how to do something about these problems, that is the time to rid ourselves of the expensive burden of schools or to reduce the function of teachers to "coaches" in the uses of machines (as Ravitch envisions). Until then, we must be more modest about this god of Technology and certainly not pin our hopes on it.

We must also, I suppose, be empathetic toward those who search with good intentions for technological panaceas. I am a teacher myself and know how hard it is to contribute toward the making of a civilized person. Can we blame those who want to find an easy way, through the agency of technology? Perhaps not. After all, it is an old quest. As early as 1918, H. L. Mencken (although completely devoid of empathy) wrote, ". . . there is no sure-cure so idiotic that some superintendent of schools will not swallow it. The aim seems to be to reduce the whole teaching process to a sort of automatic reaction, to discover some master formula that will not only take the place of competence and resourcefulness in the teacher but that will also create an artificial receptivity in the child."[8]

Mencken was not necessarily speaking of technological panaceas, but he may well have been. In the early 1920s, a teacher wrote the following poem:

Mr. Edison says
That the radio will supplant the teacher.
Already one may learn languages by means
     of Victrola records.
The moving picture will visualize
What the radio fails to get across.
Teachers will be relegated to the backwoods.
With fire-horses,

And long-haired women;
Or, perhaps shown in museums.
Education will become a matter
Of pressing the button.
Perhaps I can get a position at the switchboard.[9]

I do not go as far back as the introduction of the radio and the Victrola, but I am old enough to remember when 16-millimeter film was to be the sure cure, then closed-circuit television, then 8-millimeter film, then teacherproof textbooks. Now computers.

I know a false god when I see one.

There is still another false god that has surfaced recently, and we must not neglect it. Like the gods of Economic Utility, Consumership, and Technology, it leads us to a dead end. But unlike them, it does not merely distort or trivialize the idea of public education. It directs us to its end.

This god has several names: the god of Tribalism or Separatism; most often, in its most fervently articulated form, the god of Multiculturalism. Before saying anything about it, I should specify that it must not be confused with what has been called "cultural pluralism." Cultural pluralism is a seventy-year-old idea whose purpose is to enlarge and enrich the American Creed—specifically, to show the young how their tribal identities and narratives fit into a more inclusive and comprehensive American story. The term *multiculturalism* is sometimes used as a synonym for cultural pluralism, and in such cases, we have a semantic problem that can be clarified with relative ease. But more often than not, the term is used to denote a quite different story. In its extreme form, which is the god I will confront here, I would judge it to be a psychopathic version of cultural pluralism, and, of course, extremely dangerous. In what follows, I will put quotation marks around the term *multiculturalism* to indicate that no argument is being made against the acknowledgment of cultural differences among students. I am using the term to denote a narrative that makes cultural diversity an exclusive preoccupation.

Although this god is by no means as widely accepted as the others I have discussed, there are several states (for example, New York and Oregon) that have been deeply influenced by it and serious about urging that schooling be organized around it. Because of an expanding interest in "multiculturalism," as well as the passion of its adherents, it has been deemed dangerous enough to have provoked the distinguished historian Arthur Schlesinger, Jr., to write a refutation of it, *The Disuniting of America: Reflections on a Multicultural Society*. Although Schlesinger's book will, I believe, stand as the definitive critique of "multiculturalism," there is at least one point he does not stress enough, and which should be the beginning of any discussion of this reversion to undiluted tribalism. I refer to the fact that those who advocate a "multicultural" curriculum, especially those who speak for an Afrocentric bias, understand better than most (certainly better than, say, the U.S. Secretary of Education) the need for a god to serve; they understand that the reason why students are demoralized, bored, and distracted is not that teachers lack interesting methods and machinery but that both students and teachers lack a narrative to provide profound meaning to their lessons. It does not go too far to say that the "multiculturalists" are the most active and dedicated education philosophers we have at the moment. They are not especially interested in methods or machinery and, generally, are not competent to speak on such matters. But they have a story to tell, and they believe their story can serve as a foundation to schooling. The trouble is that it is a terrible story, at least for public schools.

Like many important narratives, this one includes concepts of good and evil. In its most frightening version, evil inheres in white people, especially those of European origin and learning. Goodness inheres in nonwhites, especially those who have been victims of "white hegemony." At least one "multiculturalist," Professor Leonard Jeffries, of City College of New York, has a biological explanation for these characteristics. He believes that the qualities of good and evil are determined by the respective quantities of melanin in the bloodstreams of different races: the more melanin, the more good; the less melanin, the more evil. One might say that this is the equivalent of the concept of Original Sin in the Christian story, with this difference: The Christian story provides a means by which Original Sin can be overcome. Jeffries's account of the source of evil leaves no opportunity for redemption.

Of course, many adherents of "multiculturalism" do not agree with Jeffries and, in any case, do not require a biological basis for believing in white, European evil. History, they argue, provides abundant reasons, most particularly in the fact of white oppression of nonwhite people. To "multiculturalists," such oppression is the key to understanding white history, literature, art, and most everything else of European origin. It follows from this that all the narratives of the white, European races are to be seen as propagandistic means of concealing their evil, or, even worse, making their evil appear virtuous. There is no possibility of proceeding in a fair-minded way, the "multiculturalists" believe, unless the narratives of white Europeans are overthrown. A particularly vigorous expression of this view is provided by four authors from the Rochester, New York, school district: "[The] legitimation of dominance, naturalization of inequality, and filtration of knowledge are being challenged in the current debate over what is 'standard' school knowledge. At issue in this debate is the struggle over accuracy versus misrepresentation, emancipatory versus hegemonic scholarship, and the constructed supremacy of Western cultural knowledge transmitted in schools versus the inherent primacy of the multiple and collective origins of knowledge."[10]

If we leave aside the vagueness, if not incomprehensibility, of such phrases as "emancipatory scholarship" and "inherent primacy," it is clear enough that the authors believe the schools are the battleground where the struggle for a new narrative must be fought. They conclude this paragraph by saying that Eurocentric knowledge must be replaced, since "[such] a singular, monovocal curriculum is one of the last institutional terrains of white, patriarchal, ruling-class hegemony."

This is clearly not the language of "cultural pluralism," which would have among its aims celebrating the struggles and achievements of nonwhite people as part of the story of humankind. In fact, the authors explicitly denounce any efforts to "heroize" (their word) such figures as Frederick Douglass, Harriet Tubman, Crispus Attucks, and Martin Luther King, Jr. They believe that the "heroizing" approach conceals the "holocaustal atrocities, economic benefits, and dehumanization of [slavery's] perpetrators." Obviously, what "multiculturalism" aims at is not reconciliation with Eurocentric history and learning, but a thorough rejection of it so that a new beginning may be made, a new narrative constructed.

In order to accomplish this, the "multiculturalists" must do two things. First, they must reveal and highlight those ugly parts of history that are usually excluded from the various Eurocentric narratives. Second, they must show that the more humane parts of those narratives have their origin in nonwhite cultures.

The first task is relatively easy, since all narratives conceal or sanitize unsavory if not indefensible chapters. Narratives are not exactly histories at all, but a special genre of story-telling that uses history to give form to ideals. "The purpose of myth," Claude Lévi-Strauss reminds us, "is to provide a model capable of overcoming a contradiction."[11] That is why no serious harm is done to the great story of Christianity by revealing that a particular Pope was an ambitious, unscrupulous schemer. Neither is it lethal to speak of the Inquisition. The reality is that there has never been a Christian—not even St. Francis or Mother Teresa—who has lived in every particular a Christian life. The story of Christianity is only in part a history of Christians. It is largely the story of the poignant struggle of people to give life to a set of transcendent ideals. That they have stumbled on the way is embarrassing and sometimes shameful, but it does not discredit the purpose of the story, which in fact is about the discrepancy between reality and the ideal.

The same is true of the American story of democracy. To point out that the Constitution, when written, permitted the exclusion of women and nonproperty owners from voting, and did not regard slaves as fully human, is not to make a mockery of the story. The creation of the Constitution, including the limitations of the men who wrote it, is only an early chapter of a two-hundred-year-old narrative whose theme is the gradual and often painful expansion of the concepts of freedom and humanity. How difficult that struggle has been was expressed by Abraham Lincoln in 1856 in a response he made to the presidential campaign of the Know-Nothing party. "Our progress in degeneracy," he observed sardonically, "appears to me pretty rapid. As a nation, we

Callslip Request 3/10/2015 7:40:07 PM

Request date:3/10/2015 12:07 PM
Request ID: 48978
Call Number:370.973 P8583
Item Barcode:

Author: Postman, Neil.
Title: End of education : redefining the value o
Enumeration:c.1Year:
Patron Name:AYU IWAOKA
Patron Barcode:

Patron comment:

Request number:

Route to:
I-Share Library:

Library Pick Up Location:

began by declaring that 'All men are created equal.' We now practically read it 'All men are created equal, *except Negroes.*' When the Know-Nothings get control, it will read 'All men are created equal, except Negroes, and foreigners, and Catholics.' "[12]

The Know-Nothings did not get control, but we know nonetheless how that reversion to degeneracy was stayed, at what cost, and how we have continued the journey that Jefferson charted. That we are far from reaching the goal is made abundantly clear by the robust complaints of those who are not yet adequately represented, including the "multiculturalists." But the point is that it is possible, by ignoring its transcendent ideals, to tell America's story as a history of racism, inequity, and violence. Is this the story we wish to be the foundation of American public schooling? If the answer is, Yes, because it contains truth, then we must turn to the second task of the "multiculturalists" to see if they are mainly concerned with truth-telling. That task is to show that the humane parts of the Eurocentric narrative have their origins in nonwhite cultures. Schlesinger's book documents the failure of "multiculturalists" to come even close to the truth. He shows that according to respected historians, including black historians, most of the claims made by "multiculturalists" are propagandistic fantasies. These include the claims that black Africa is where science, philosophy, religion, medicine, technology, and other great humanistic achievements originated; that ancient Egyptians were black; that Pythagoras and Aristotle stole their mathematics and philosophies from black scholars in Egypt; that most American blacks originated in Egypt; and that the enlightened parts of the U.S. Constitution were based, in some measure, on political principles borrowed from the Iroquois. Schlesinger is so discouraged by the abuse of history reflected in these claims that he concludes:

"If some Kleagle of the Ku Klux Klan wanted to devise an educational curriculum for the specific purpose of handicapping and disabling black Americans, he would not be likely to come up with anything more diabolically effective than Afrocentrism."[13]

One might reply to Schlesinger that neither historical balance nor truth is the issue here. What is being attempted is the creation of a new narrative, similar in point and method to the process by which, for example, American colonists constructed a mythology of the Pilgrims as democratic nation-builders. In that instance, history was used, invented, or forgotten to suit the needs of the story. The story, as we know, has been hugely successful. Americans know about Miles Standish but not about Squanto and Wituwamet. Americans celebrate, even revere, Thanksgiving, but they do not know (or, if they do, give it little weight) that some Indians call Thanksgiving the National Day of Mourning.

Of course, it is not irrelevant to ask how much truth or falsehood is contained in any narrative. A narrative constructed mostly out of falsehoods usually fails, leaving its adherents bitter and, as Schlesinger reminds us, ignorant. But even if we make a most generous assessment of the facts that form the core of the "multicultural" story, we are left with the question, Can it work?

I believe it cannot, for several reasons. The first is of a practical nature. Why should the public, which is largely of European origin, support a school program that takes as its theme their own evil? Would nonwhites support a public school whose curriculum proceeds from the assumption that nonwhites are inferior? And if the "multiculturalists" reply, That is exactly what happens in most schools, then the remedy is to revise the story so that it allows children of all races to find a dignified place for themselves in it. It is true enough

that whites have oppressed blacks, but blacks have oppressed other blacks, and even whites; and whites have
oppressed other whites; and Indians have slaughtered whites,
and whites, Indians; and Europeans have oppressed Asians,
and Asians, Europeans. How far shall we go with this?

If I may amend Niels Bohr's remark, cited earlier, the opposite of a profound story is another profound story, by
which I mean that the story of every group may be told in-
spiringly, without excluding its blemishes but with an emphasis on the various struggles to achieve humanity, or, to
borrow from Lincoln again, the struggles to reveal the better
angels of our nature. This is what once was meant by cultural
pluralism.

The argument is sometimes made that a "multicultural"
curriculum is justified where an entire student population is
African-American (or Mexican or Puerto Rican), as is often
the case in our large cities. This might make sense if it were
the task of the public schools to create a public of hyphenated
Americans. But our students already come to school as hyphenated Americans. The task of the public schools, properly
conceived, is to erase the hyphens or to make them less dis-
tinct. The idea of a public school is not to make blacks black,
or Koreans Korean, or Italians Italian, but to make Americans.
The alternative leads, quite obviously, to the "Balkanization"
of public schools—which is to say, their end. An Afrocentric
curriculum for Afro-Americans? Then why not a Sinocentric
curriculum for the Chinese? An Italocentric curriculum for
Italians? A Judeocentric curriculum for Jews? A Teutocentric
for Germans? A Graecocentric for Greeks?

This path not only leads to the privatizing of schooling but
to a privatizing of the mind, and it makes the creation of a
public mind quite impossible. The theme of schooling would
then be divisiveness, not sameness, and would inevitably en-

gender hate. In December 1993, Minister Louis Farrakhan gave a talk in Madison Square Garden, during which he made reference to a young African-American man who had, only a few days before, been arrested for gunning down passengers on the Long Island Railroad. Most of the victims were white; a few were Asians. Although there is no evidence that Farrakhan encouraged their response, members of the audience cheered either the young man or his deed. It is not clear which. One may explain this response by reference to a sense of generalized rage on the part of African-Americans against European culture. If that is the case, then surely the role of the public school is not to intensify it, but to help create a sane alternative to it.

4 · Gods That May Serve

Who writes the songs that young girls sing? Or the tales that old men tell? Who creates the myths that bind a nation and give purpose and meaning to the idea of a public education? In America, it is the advertisers and, of course, the popular musicians and filmmakers; maybe even the hollow men gathered around swimming pools in Beverly Hills, inventing stories we call television sitcoms.

This does not exhaust the list, but teachers are not on it. It must be clear at the beginning that schools have not and have never been organized to create forceful, inspiring narratives. They collect them, amplify them, distribute them, ennoble them. They sometimes refute them, mock them, or neglect them. But they create nothing, and this is, I suppose, as it should be. As those who would privatize schooling correctly point out, our public schools are state-run agencies and have no license to reconstruct society on their own authority; they are given neither permission nor encouragement to promote a worldview that has no resonance in the society at large. Schools, we might say, are mirrors of social belief, giving back what citizens put in front of them. But they are not fixed in one position. They can be moved up and down and sideways, so that at different times and in different venues, they will reflect one thing and not another. But always they show something that is *there*, not of the schools' invention, but of the society that pays for the schools and uses them for various purposes. This is why the gods of Economic Utility, Consumership, Technology, and Separatism are to be found in our schools now, exerting their force and commanding allegiance. They are gods that come from outside the walls of the classroom.

All of this must be quite obvious, and a reader may well ask, When did the coauthor of a book called *Teaching as a Subversive Activity* grasp the point? As Joseph Heller might say it, I never didn't grasp the point. I understood, in 1969, as now, that at any given time in the symbolic universe of a community, there dwell multiple narratives—some shining at the forefront, vivid and unmistakable; some in the background, indistinct and half-forgotten; some sleeping, some recently awakened, and many in uneasy contradiction to others. If an author wishes to define teaching as a subversive activity, he is inventing no god, but merely calling upon one to take precedence over another. For in this case, our citizens believe in two contradictory reasons for schooling. One is that schools must teach the young to accept the world as it is, with all of their culture's rules, requirements, constraints, and even prejudices. The other is that the young should be taught to be critical thinkers, so that they become men and women of independent mind, distanced from the conventional wisdom of their own time and with strength and skill enough to change what is wrong.

Each of these beliefs is part of a unique narrative that tells of what it means to be human, what it means to be a citizen, what it means to be intelligent. And each of these narratives can be found in American tradition. An author may think it necessary to subordinate one to the other—or vice versa—depending on what seems needed at a particular time. That is why, having coauthored *Teaching as a Subversive Activity*, he might later on write *Teaching as a Conserving Activity*.

The problem, as always, is: What is needed now? My argument, beginning with the title of this book, is that the narratives that underlie our present conception of school do not serve us well and may lead to the end of public schooling— "end" meaning its conversion to privatized schooling (as Henry Perkinson predicts in his updated version of *The Imperfect Panacea*) or its subordination to individually controlled technology (as Lewis Perelman predicts in *School's Out*). It is also possible that schooling will be taken over by corporations (as, for example, in the way Chris Whittle proposes) and operated entirely on principles associated with a market economy.

Any or all of these are possibilities. But this book takes no great interest in any of these plans, including the option of public school choice as advocated by Seymour Fliegel (in his book *Miracle in East Harlem*). These are essentially engineering matters. They are about the practical, efficient way to deliver school services. They are important but barely touch the question, What are schools for? Yes, it matters if parents have a choice of schools, if schools are smaller, if class size is reduced, if money is available to hire more teachers, if some students receive public funds to attend private schools. But are we not still left with the question, *Why?* What is all the sound and fury and expense about? If a metaphor may be permitted, we can make the trains run on time, but if they do not go where we want them to go, why bother?

My intention here is to offer an answer in the form of five narratives that, singly and in concert, contain sufficient resonance and power to be taken seriously as reasons for schooling. They offer, I believe, moral guidance, a sense of continuity, explanations of the past, clarity to the present, hope for the future. They come as close to a sense of transcendence as I can imagine within the context of public schooling.

I am, of course, aware that what I shall propose, to put the mildest face on it, is presumptuous. For I must not only put forward ideas that inspire me but ideas calculated to inspire the young, their teachers, and their parents. My own heart and mind, I know well enough. Can I claim the same knowledge of the hearts and minds of my countrymen and -women? I cannot be sure. Who can? But I do not proceed in a state of wild surmise. I have, for example, tested these ideas in scores of places with parents and teachers from Oregon to Connecticut, with students from grammar school through the university level. I've listened to what they have said and, just as carefully, to what they have not said. When I have previously written about any of these ideas, I have learned, from what readers have in turn written me, the arguments for them and against them. I have spent thirty years as an affectionate critic of American prejudices, tastes, and neuroses and have been astonished and pleased to discover I share most of them. By this, I do not mean I can speak for Americans, only about them. I have also gained some confidence in these judgments from many lectures in Europe, discovering, without surprise, that Alexis de Tocqueville was right: Americans are different—in some ways better, in some worse—but different. And when one is in a foreign land, the differences emerge with uncommon clarity.

I mention all of this not as a warranty of the soundness of my proposals but as assurance that they are grounded in a focused conception of those for whom they are intended. I think I know what gods are possible in America and what gods are not. Otherwise, there would be no point in proceeding.

If you judge what follows to be unrealistic, superficial, or

otherwise unsound, Part II of this book will, indeed, be pointless. But if you agree that these ideas move us in the right direction, Part II will provide specific examples of how one
might bring these ideas to life, and the implications of doing
so. The detail I will provide in Part II leads me to be as brief
as possible in describing the narratives that follow. There is,
in any case, nothing astonishing about them. Each is part of
our symbolic landscape. We talk about them. We wonder
about them. We sometimes forget about them. But they are
there, and the question is, Can we use them to provide an
end—that is, a purpose—to schooling?

The Spaceship Earth

Not long ago, I found myself in an extended conversation
with Marvin Minsky, the distinguished scientist who is famous (some say notorious) for his passionate advocacy of
"artificial intelligence."[1] In providing a context for his fertile
imagination, Minsky referred to the influence on his thinking
of several science-fiction writers, remarking that science-
fiction writers are our true philosophers. It is significant, I
thought, that he failed to include among a rather extensive
list Mary Shelley (*Frankenstein*), Aldous Huxley (*Brave New
World*), George Orwell (*1984*), and Ray Bradbury (*Fahrenheit
451*). I will come to these gloomy philosophers later on, but
surely Minsky has a point, and I wish to pursue it by focusing
on the most popular of all our science-fiction philosophers,
Steven Spielberg. Spielberg is sometimes near-Homeric in his
capacity to give form to myths that resonate deeply, especially with our youth. I put aside, for the moment, *Jurassic
Park* (which connects him with the tradition of *Frankenstein*)
and *Schindler's List* (in which he forgoes the prophetic tradi-

tion altogether) and refer to *Close Encounters of the Third Kind* and *E.T.*, each of which asks us to believe that we are not alone in the universe. Perhaps we are, perhaps not; most likely, we will never know. But what his stories make clear is that from both a metaphorical and a literal point of view the Earth is a spaceship and we are its crew members.

This is by no means an original idea, but, unlike, for example, H. G. Wells or Jules Verne, who also wrote on this subject, Spielberg puts the idea in a form that is essentially religious, or at least spiritual; that is to say, he does not merely excite our imaginations about our Spaceship Earth. He insists on our moral obligation to it. Anyone who has talked to young people about either of these films will know how clearly they grasp the sense of responsibility urged on them, as well as how deeply runs their emotional response to the idea that we can no longer take for granted the well-being of the planet.

We have here, then, a narrative of extraordinary potential: the story of human beings as stewards of the Earth, caretakers of a vulnerable space capsule. It is a relatively new narrative, not fully developed and fraught with uncertainties and even contradictions. (For example, I hesitate to invoke the image of the starship *Enterprise* from *Star Trek*, because for all its dramatic appeal, Captain Kirk is essentially a benevolent tyrant, democracy being rejected as an appropriate form of social organization for penetrating the "final frontier.") Nonetheless, the story of Spaceship Earth has the power to bind people. It makes the idea of racism both irrelevant and ridiculous, and it makes clear the interdependence of human beings and their need for solidarity. If any part of the spaceship is poisoned, then all suffer—which is to say that the extinction of the rain forest is not a Brazilian problem; the pollution of the oceans is not a Miami problem; the depletion of the ozone layer is not an Australian problem. It follows from this, of course, that genocide is not a Bosnian problem, hunger not a Somalian problem, political oppression not a Chinese problem. "Never send to know for whom the bell tolls," wrote John Donne. "It tolls for thee." If ever there was a narrative to animate that idea, the Earth as our one and only spaceship is it.

Moreover, I need hardly point out that this form of global consciousness does not significantly conflict with any traditional religious beliefs. I am not aware of any deity who would take satisfaction in the destruction of the Earth, or, for that matter, the disintegration of cities, or hostility among people holding different points of view. One can be a Christian, a Muslim, a Taoist, a Jew, or a Buddhist and yet be imbued with a commitment to the preservation of the planet. In like fashion, the story of the Earth as a spaceship does not conflict with national or tribal tales; it does not require that one reject or even be indifferent to one's national, regional, or tribal loyalties. One can be an American, or a Norwegian, or a Frenchman, or, for that matter, a Lapp and, without sacrificing one's identity, can be enlarged by adopting the role of Earth's caretaker.

One can, that is, unless driven by a competing narrative which insists that one's own nation is all that counts in Heaven and Earth. As I write, at least one school system in the state of Florida has adopted a story requiring teachers and students to believe that the United States is superior to all other nations—one assumes, in all respects. A similar story has been proposed in New York City (but, for the moment, rejected). This is an idea that calls to mind the desperate efforts of the Queen in *Snow White and the Seven Dwarfs* to reassure herself of her preeminent and unfailing beauty. "Mirror, mirror on the wall," she daily asks, "who is the fairest one of all?" But in that case, the mirror tells the truth, thus putting poor

Snow White in harm's way. It is a terrible burden to place on children to require them to ask this question about nationhood and of a mirror that is programmed in advance always to reply, "America, America." In addition to its being a perversion of the American Creed, such a story is a sign of a desperate quest for a meaningful narrative, and one's sympathies must be extended to those who conceived of this. It is, nonetheless, doubtful that its disoriented authors can find the Earth as spaceship an acceptable narrative. But, I believe, many will, for this is an idea whose time has come. It is a story of interdependence and global cooperation, of what is at the core of humanness; a story that depicts waste and indifference as evil, that requires a vision of the future and a commitment to the present. In this story, if the students ask, "Mirror, mirror on the wall, which is the fairest of us all?," the mirror replies, "This is a pretty stupid question. Have you not noticed that you are all on the same ship? That you must rely on each other to survive, and that you have not taken sufficient care of your home?"

The Fallen Angel

I use a religious metaphor here to emphasize the point that what I shall describe is not merely a method or an epistemology but a narrative, and one of almost universal acceptance. The story as it is told in various places and forms is essentially a religious idea, and I trust that this fact, by itself, will turn no one away. Most serious narratives are rooted in a spiritual or metaphysical idea, even those narratives—inductive science, for example—that are suspicious of metaphysics. In fact, as I shall have occasion to say in a moment, science is more committed to the story of the fallen angel than any other system of belief.

This is the story: If perfection is to be found anyplace in the universe, it is assumed to exist in God or gods. There may have been a time when human beings were perfect, but at some point, for various reasons, their powers were diminished, so that they must live forever in a state of imperfect understanding. Indeed, for us to believe that we are godlike, or perfect, is among the most serious sins of which we are capable. The Greeks called the sin "hubris." The Christians call it "pride." Scientists call it "dogmatism."

The major theme of the story is that human beings make mistakes. All the time. It is our nature to make mistakes. We can scarcely let an hour go by without making one. "I beseech you, in the bowels of Christ," Oliver Cromwell pleaded, "think it possible that you may be mistaken." That we may be mistaken, and probably are, is the meaning of the "fall" in the fallen angel. The meaning of "angel" is that we are capable of correcting our mistakes, provided we proceed without hubris, pride, or dogmatism; provided that we accept our cosmic status as the error-prone species. Therein lies the possibility of our redemption: Knowing that we do not know and cannot know the whole truth, we may move toward it inch by inch by discarding what we know to be false. And then watch the truth move further and further away. It is a sad story, to be sure; its melancholy poignancy is captured in the myth of Sisyphus, the story of Job, and scores of other tales the world over. It is a noble story, as well, and a funny one, its humor expressed in the wise Yiddish saying, *Man tracht un Got lacht* ("Man thinks and God laughs"). The saying tells us exactly where we stand, as do the famous lines of Omar in *The Rubáiyát:* "The Moving Finger writes; and having writ /

Moves on: nor all your piety nor wit / Shall lure it back to cancel half a Line / Nor all your Tears wash out a Word of it." And yet the struggle goes on, does it not?

The most explicit and sophisticated example of how this narrative improves the human condition is, of course, science. This would hardly be worth noting except for the fact that in the popular mind, and certainly in school, science is thought to be something other than a method for correcting our mistakes—namely, a source of ultimate truth. Such a belief is, in itself, an instance of the sin of pride, and no self-respecting scientist will admit to holding it. "The scientific method," Thomas Henry Huxley once wrote, "is nothing but the normal working of the human mind." That is to say, when the mind is working; that is to say further, when it is engaged in correcting its mistakes.

Taking this point of view, we may conclude that science is not physics, biology, or chemistry—is not even a "subject"—but a moral imperative drawn from a larger narrative whose purpose is to give perspective, balance, and humility to learning.

It is strange, then, that there are scientists who, putting aside their acceptance of uncertainty in their "subject," are true and unshakable believers in some social or political doctrine; stranger still that there are devout individuals who, knowing fully of their fall, believe nonetheless that their understanding has penetrated the will of their god. We have here a mystery that goes to the heart of education. How can we explain the quest for certainty, which is so easily converted to an unseemly, unjustified, and often lethal dogmatism? This is the question John Dewey struggled with, as well as Bertrand Russell and scores of other modern education philosophers, including those who answer, "Teach critical thinking," without having the faintest idea of how that might be done or giving any thought to the psychological sources of the opposition to it. It is the question Jacob Bronowski addressed in his monumental project, both a television series and a book, called *The Ascent of Man*. Although deeply religious, Bronowski forgoes, at the start, use of a religious metaphor and turns to Werner Heisenberg's Principle of Uncertainty as a narrative to give meaning to the idea that all human knowledge is limited. The principle states that the act of discovering the velocity of an electron changes its position, and vice versa, so that we can never know both the position and velocity at the same time. Although referring to subatomic events, the principle is often used as a metaphor for the fundamental uncertainty of all human knowledge. But Bronowski prefers the phrase The Principle of Tolerance, because, he says, though there may be knowledge of which we can be sure, such knowledge is always confined within a certain tolerance—meaning, within some limited sphere. Yes, we know things, but much of it is wrong, and what replaces that may be wrong as well. And even that which is right, and seems to need no amendment, is limited in its scope and its applicability.

In the last program of his television series, Bronowski is seen standing in a pond on the grounds of the old Auschwitz concentration camp. Near-overwrought by what Auschwitz symbolizes, he resorts, as so many have done before him, to a religious metaphor. "Into this pond," he says, "were flushed the ashes of some four million people. And that was not done by gas. It was done by arrogance. It was done by dogma. . . . When people believe that they have absolute knowledge . . . this is how they behave. This is what men do when they aspire to the knowledge of gods."[2]

At the end, and after having reviewed the entire history of humanity's struggle to discover knowledge, Bronowski offers a single lesson: We must cure ourselves of the itch for absolute knowledge. How to do this, is the question. A course in "critical thinking" is surely not an answer. An increase in the number of science courses is even less of an answer. The Germans once had the most rigorous science program in the world, and produced true-believing Nazis. The Russians, later, were almost a match, and produced true-believing Communists. The quest for certainty, for absolute authority, cannot be stayed by courses or curriculum afterthoughts. But suppose the purpose of school was to cure the itch for absolute knowledge. Suppose we took seriously the idea that we are dangerous to ourselves and others when we aspire to the knowledge of the gods. What then?

The American Experiment

All children enter school as question marks and leave as periods. It is an old saying, but still useful in thinking about how schooling is normally conducted. It is also applicable, in various forms, to other situations and institutions. For example, we might say all nations begin as question marks and end as exclamation points. This must have been the way some Florida patriots were thinking when they made it obligatory for schools to teach that America is superior to all other countries. Someone obviously feels that the American Creed is an exclamation point, a finished product, a settled issue. But this version of the meaning of America, assuming anyone could actually believe it, leads directly to the kind of blindness that Bronowski warns against. Even worse, it gives dogmatism a bad name.

Every school, save those ripped asunder by separatist ideology, tries to tell a story about America that will enable students to feel a sense of national pride. Students deserve that, and their parents expect it. The question is how to do this and yet avoid indifference, on the one hand, and a psychopathic nationalism, on the other.

As it happens, there is such a story available to us. It has the virtues of being largely true, of explaining our past, including our mistakes, of inviting participation in the present, of offering hope for the future. It is a story that does not require the belief that America is superior to all other countries, only that it is unique, youthful, admirable, and opened wide to unfulfilled humane possibilities. No student can ask more of his or her country. No school can offer more.

I propose, then, the story of America as an experiment, a perpetual and fascinating question mark. The story includes the experience of those who lived here before the European invasion, and of those Europeans who provided the invaders with both their troubles and their ideas. After all, every story has a prologue. But the story properly begins, as Abraham Lincoln saw it, with a series of stunning and dangerous questions. Is it possible to have a government of the people, by the people, and for the people? And who are the people, anyway? And how shall they proceed in governing themselves? And how shall we protect individuals from the power of the people? And why should we do all this in the first place?

Any reader of this book will know of these questions, and many more. It is not my intention to give a history lesson. My intention is to make the point that these questions are still unanswered and will always remain so. The American Constitution is not a catechism, but a hypothesis. It is less the law of the land than an expression of the lay of the land as it has been understood by various people at different times. Stephen Carter, a law professor at Yale University, in his book *The Culture of Disbelief*, argues with one widespread view of what is meant by the statement "Congress shall make no law respecting an establishment of religion or prohibiting the free exercise thereof." He claims that the purpose of this provision is to protect religion from the state, not the state from religion, as so many seem to think. On June 29, 1994, the *New York Times* carried on its first page an account of a Supreme Court decision on this very matter, in which, in effect, six judges disagreed with Carter and three agreed. Maybe next time the score will be different. Scores are important, but not as important as the process that produces them, a point of view that should surprise no one, since America was the first nation to be argued into existence. The Declaration of Independence is an argument, and was composed as such. Tom Paine's *The Rights of Man* is an argument, and, in fact, one with serious flaws (not nearly as cogent an argument, I've always thought, as the argument—by Edmund Burke—it was intended to refute). All Supreme Court decisions are arguments, including some deeply embarrassing ones—for example, the Dred Scott decision, which calls to mind the Lincoln-Douglas debates, our best-known and possibly our most skillfully crafted arguments. Of course, I do not mean to suggest that all our arguments have been made by people of the quality of Jefferson, Paine, and Lincoln. The idea, from the beginning, was to allow everyone to participate in the arguments, provided they were not slaves, women, or excessively poor (although it is hard to imagine how anyone could have been poorer than Tom Paine). Through argument (or more precisely, the cessation of argument) the slaves were freed and admitted to participation, and their progeny are now among our most vigorous arguers; then women; then the poor; and more recently, students and homosexuals and even, God help us, radio talk-show hosts.

Our history allows us to claim that the basic question

posed by the American experiment is: Can a nation be formed, maintained, and preserved on the principle of continuous argumentation? The emphasis is as much on "continuous" as on "argumentation." We know what happens when argument ceases—blood happens, as in our Civil War, when we stopped arguing with one another; or in several other wars, when we stopped arguing with other people; or in a war or two when, perhaps, no argument was possible.

Of course, all the arguments have a theme that is made manifest in a series of questions: What is freedom? What are its limits? What is a human being? What are the obligations of citizenship? What is meant by democracy? And so on. Happily, Americans are neither the only nor the first people to argue these questions, which means we have found answers, and may continue to find them, in the analects of Confucius, the commandments of Moses, the dialogues of Plato, the aphorisms of Jesus, the instructions of the Koran, the speeches of Milton, the plays of Shakespeare, the essays of Voltaire, the prophecies of Hegel, the manifestos of Marx, the sermons of Martin Luther King, Jr., and any other source where such questions have been seriously addressed. But which ones are the right answers? We don't know. There's the rub, and the beauty and the value of the story. So we argue and experiment and complain, and grieve, and rejoice, and argue some more, without end. Which means that in this story we need conceal nothing from ourselves; no shame need endure forever; no accomplishment merits excessive pride. All is fluid and subject to change, to better arguments, to the results of future experiments.

This, it seems to me, is a fine and noble story to offer as a reason for schooling: to provide our youth with the knowledge and will to participate in the great experiment; to teach them how to argue, and to help them discover what questions are worth arguing about; and, of course, to make sure they know what happens when arguments cease. No one is excluded from the story. Every group has made good arguments, and bad ones. All points of view are admissible. The only thing we have to fear is that someone will insist on putting in an exclamation point when we are not yet finished. Like in Florida.

The Law of Diversity

America has always been a nation of nations, our schools always multicultural. But educators have not always been concerned to emphasize this fact, in part because of the belief that through schooling a common culture could be created; in part because immigrant cultures were thought to be inferior to Anglo-Saxon cultures. The second idea is in justifiable disgrace. The first is still functional, as reflected, for example, in the popularity of the idea of "cultural literacy," as developed by E. D. Hirsch, Jr. He argues that the role of schooling is to create a common culture but that we cannot have one unless our citizens share a common core of knowledge—that is, *facts*, about history, literature, science, philosophy, wars, cities, popular arts. After consulting with appropriate experts in a variety of fields, Hirsch took the trouble to list thousands of names, places, and events that comprise the store of facts of a "culturally literate" person. He insists that most of these be given attention in the course of our children's schooling. I have, in another place, criticized Hirsch's project on several grounds, among them his indifference to providing meaning to schooling, and the clear impossibility in an "information age" of making such a list without being maddeningly arbitrary. For almost every item on Hirsch's list, there are at least ten others that are not on it and whose importance can be argued with equal justification. In other words, Hirsch's list is not a solution to the problem of how to create a common culture, but an unintentional expression of the problem itself. That is why in this book, which is also concerned with how to form a common culture, I have placed little emphasis on what facts can be known, much on what narratives can be believed. (In providing our children with a sense of meaning, we would do much better to take as a guide Schindler's list than Hirsch's list.)

But one thing may be said clearly in Hirsch's defense. His list is no argument against diversity. It is, in fact, a celebration of diversity. Even a casual perusal of the list will reveal that it includes names, places, events, and ideas from all over the world, and implies significant artistic, intellectual, and social contributions from diverse ethnic groups. To the extent that Hirsch's list is intended for American students, its diversity was inevitable.

The idea of diversity is a rich narrative around which to organize the schooling of the young. But there are right reasons to do this, and wrong ones. The worst possible reason, as I have already discussed, is to use the fact of ethnic diversity to inspire a curriculum of revenge; that is, for a group that has been oppressed to try to even the score with the rest of America by singling itself out for excessive praise and attention. Although the impulse to revenge is in itself understandable, such a view will lead to weird falsifications, divisiveness, and isolation. There is a joke about this that Jews tell to each other about themselves: One day, in a small town in Russia, circa 1900, a Jew notices many people in panic, running this way and that, shouting for help. He stops another Jew and asks what is happening. He is told that there is a circus in town and the lions have escaped from their cages. "Is this good or bad for the Jews?" he asks.

The joke is intended to mock a self-absorbed attitude that allows for no larger identification than with one's own group. One may as well ask, Is Shakespeare good for the Jews? Are Newton's laws good for the Jews? There are, to be sure, certain Jewish sects whose answer to these questions is, in fact, "bad the Jews," because secular learning of any sort is considered a distraction from Talmudic studies, and a threat to piety. But that is exactly the point. Such sects have their own schools and their own narratives, and wish to keep their young away from public education. Any education that promotes a near-exclusive concern with one's own group may have value, but is hostile to the idea of a public education and to the growth of a common culture. Certainly, there may be occasions when it is natural and appropriate to ask, for example, Was this good or bad for blacks, or Latinos, or Koreans? But the point of the joke is that if everything is seen through the lens of ethnicity, then isolation, parochialness, and hostility, not to mention absurdity, are the inevitable result.

There is, in addition, another reason for emphasizing diversity, one of which we may be skeptical. I refer to the psychological argument that claims the self-esteem of some students may be raised by focusing their attention on the accomplishments of those of their own kind, especially if the teachers are of their own kind. I cannot say if this is so or not, but it needs to be pointed out that while a diminished self-esteem is no small matter, one of the main purposes of public education—it is at the core of a common culture—is the idea that students must esteem something other than self. This is a point Cornel West has stressed in addressing both whites and blacks. For example, after reviewing the pernicious effects of race consciousness, which include poverty and paranoia, he ends his book *Race Matters* by saying, "We simply cannot enter the twenty-first century at each other's throats. . . . We are at a crucial crossroads in the history of this nation—and we either hang together by combating these forces that divide and degrade us or we hang separately."[3] I take this to be a heartfelt plea for the necessity of providing ourselves and especially our young with a comprehensive narrative that makes a constructive and unifying use of diversity.

Fortunately, there is such a narrative. It has both a theoretical and a practical component, which gives it special force. The theoretical component comes to us from science, expressed rather abstractly in the Second Law of Thermodynamics. The law tells us that although matter can be neither created nor destroyed (the First Law), it tends toward becoming useless. The name given to this tendency is entropy, which means that everything in the universe moves inexorably toward sameness, and when matter reaches a state in which there is no differentiation, there is no employable energy. This would be a rather relentlessly depressing notion if not for the fact that there are "negentropic" forces in the universe, energies that retard sameness and keep things moving, organized, and (from a human point of view) useful. Every time we clean our homes, or our streets, or use information to solve a problem, or make a schedule, we are combating entropy, using intelligence and energy to overcome (that is, postpone) the inevitable decay of organization.

The physicists describe all of this in mathematical codes and do not always appreciate the ways in which the rest of us employ their ideas of entropy and negentropy. Still, the universe is as much our business as it is theirs, and if there are lessons to be learned from the universe, attention must be paid. The lesson here is that sameness is the enemy of vitality and creativity. From a practical point of view, we can see this in every field of human activity. Stagnation occurs when nothing new and different comes from outside the system. The English language is a superb example of this point; so is Latin. English is a relatively young language, not much more than six hundred years old (assuming Chaucer to be our first major English author). It began its journey as a Teutonic tongue, changed itself by admitting the French language, then Italian, and then welcomed new words and forms from wherever its speakers moved around the globe. T. S. Eliot once remarked that English is the best language for a poet to use, since it contains, for the poet's choice, the rhythms of many languages. This is an arguable point, perhaps. But it is not arguable that English is rapidly becoming the global language, has more words in it, by far, than any other language, and exerts its influence everywhere (much to the chagrin of the French, who, failing to grasp the importance of diversity, are using their energies to prevent changes in their language). English, in a word, is the most diverse language on earth, and because of that, its vitality and creativity are assured. Latin, on the other hand, is dead. It is dead because it is no longer open to change, especially change from outside itself. Those who speak and write it, speak and write it as has been done for centuries. Other languages drew upon Latin for strength, picked on its flesh and bones, created themselves from its nourishment. But Latin was not nourished in return, which is why its usefulness is so limited.

Whenever a language or an art form becomes fixed in time and impermeable, drawing only on its own resources, it is punished by entropy. Whenever difference is allowed, the result is growth and strength. There is no art form flourishing today, or that has flourished in the past, that has not done so on the wings of diversity—American musicians borrowing from African rhythms, South American architects employing Scandinavian ideas, German painters finding inspiration in Egyptian art, French filmmakers influenced by Japanese techniques.

We even find the law of diversity operating in the genetic information we pass on when procreating. In cases where marriage is confined to those of the same family—where people, as it were, clone themselves—entropic defects are more likely to occur than when differences are admitted. We may go so far as to say that sameness is the enemy not only of vitality but of excellence, for where there are few or no differences—in genetic structure, in language, in art—it is not possible to develop robust standards of excellence. I am aware that there are those who have come to the opposite conclusion. They argue that diversity in human affairs makes it impossible to have a standard of anything because there are too many points of view, too many different traditions, too many purposes; thus, diversity, they conclude, makes relativists of us all.

At a theoretical level, we may have an interesting argument here. But from a practical point of view, we can see how diversity works to provide an enriched sense of excellence. During the weeks of the latest World Cup tournament, nations from every part of the world were participating—Nigeria, Saudi Arabia, Morocco, Cameroon, Argentina, Brazil, Germany, Italy, and many others. Each team brought a special tradition and a unique style to the games. The Germans were methodical and efficient, the Brazilians flamboyant, the Italians emotional. They were all good but different, and they all knew what "good" means. The Americans didn't have much of a style and even less of a tradition, and though they played bravely, they were eliminated fairly early. I am not aware of their complaining that they lost because they have a different standard of "good." (For example, the team that scores the fewest goals wins.) Indeed, such a claim would be demeaning to them, as it would be demeaning to Japanese or Peruvian artists to say that their works are so different from those of other traditions that no judgments can be made of them. Their works, of course, are different from others, but what that means is not that excellence becomes meaningless but that the rest of the world expands and enriches its ideas of "good." At the same time, because we are all human, our expanded ideas of "good" are apt to be comprehensible and recognizable. In painting, we look for delicacy, simplicity, feeling, craftsmanship, originality, symmetry, all of which are aspirations of painters all over the world, as character, insight, believability, and emotion are aspirations of playwrights. No one faults Arthur Miller for failing to use iambic pentameter in writing *Death of a Salesman*. But what makes his play "good" is not so different from what makes *Macbeth* "good." Diversity does not mean the disintegration of standards, is not an argument against standards, does not lead to a chaotic, irresponsible relativism. It is an argument for the growth and malleability of standards, a growth that takes place across time and space and that is given form by differences of gender, religion, and all the other categories of humanity.

Thus, the story of how language, art, politics, science, and most expressions of human activity have grown, been vitalized and enriched through the intermingling of different ideas is one way to organize learning and to provide the young with a sense of pride in being human. In this story, we do not read Gabriel García Márquez to make Hispanic students happy, but because of the excellence of his novels. That Emily Dickinson and Edna St. Vincent Millay were women is not irrelevant, but we ask students to know their work because their poems are good, not to strike a blow for feminism. We read Whitman and Langston Hughes for the same reason, not because the former was a homosexual and the latter African-American. Do we learn about Einstein because he was Jewish? Marie Curie because she was Polish? Aristotle because he was Greek? Confucius because he was Chinese? Cervantes because he was handicapped? Do we listen to the music of Grieg because he was a short Norwegian, or Beethoven because he was a deaf German? In the story of diversity, we do not learn of these people to advance a political agenda or to raise the level of students' self-esteem. We learn about these people for two reasons: because they demonstrate how the vitality and creativity of humanity depend on diversity, and because they have set the standards to which civilized people adhere. The law of diversity thus makes intelligent humans of us all.

The Word Weavers/The World Makers

I once had the good fortune to attend a lecture by Elizabeth Eisenstein, author of a monumental two-volume study of the printing press as an agent of cultural change. During the question period, she was asked how she had come by her interest in the subject. She appeared to welcome the question. She told the audience that when she was a sixth-grade student, her teacher remarked that the invention of the printing press with movable type represented one of the great advances of human civilization, almost the equal of the invention of speech itself. Young Elizabeth took this remark to heart. But then a strange thing happened—in a word, nothing. The subject was never mentioned again. It did not come up in junior high school, senior high school, or college. Fortunately, it remained in her mind during all that time, and the result was that she eventually devoted herself to a detailed explication of what her sixth-grade teacher must have meant.

That such a thing could happen is at once startling and yet unsurprising. School is notorious for neglecting to mention, let alone study, some of the more important events in human history. In fact, something quite similar to what happened to Elizabeth Eisenstein happened to me when I was in Mrs. Soybel's fifth-grade class. In that class, considerable attention was paid to public speaking, especially pronunciation, since the school was in Brooklyn, New York, and it was generally believed (and still is) that people from Brooklyn do not pronounce their words correctly. One of my classmates, Gerald Melnikoff, was whispering and mumbling his weekly oral presentation and thereby aroused Mrs. Soybel's pedagogical wrath. She told Gerald that he was speaking as if he had marbles in his mouth; then, addressing the rest of the class, she told us that language was God's greatest gift to humanity. Our ability to speak, she said, was what made us human, and this we must never forget. I took the remark seriously. (I recall that for some reason I was even frightened by it.) But as with Elizabeth Eisenstein and the printing press, the matter was never mentioned again, certainly not by Mrs. Soybel. She gave us excellent lessons in spelling, grammar, and writing and taught us to remove the marbles from our mouths when we spoke. But the role of language in making us human disappeared. I didn't hold this against her—after all, she did mention the idea—but I waited for the subject to come up again in junior high, senior high, and college. I waited in vain. Whenever language was discussed, it was done so within the context of its being a useful tool—definitely not as a gift from God, and not even as a tool that makes us human.

Of course, one does not need to call on God, either literally or metaphorically, to tell the story of language and humanness, of human beings as the word weavers of the planet. This does not mean the story is without mystery. No one knows, for example, when we began to speak. Was it 50,000 years ago, or 100,000 years, or longer? No one even knows *why* we began to speak. The usual answer is that speech arose exclusively as a functional mechanism; that is, without speech, the species could not have survived. Someone absolutely had to learn to say, "The tiger is hiding behind the tree!" But Susanne Langer thought otherwise.[4] Something happened to our brains, she believed, that created in us a need to transform the world through symbols. Perhaps to give us something interesting to do in our spare time, or for the sheer aesthetic joy of it. We became symbol makers, not to spare us from the teeth of the tiger but for some other reason, which remains mysterious. Of course, we eventually discovered how speech could assist us in survival, but that was not the reason we began to speak to ourselves and to others. I place speaking to ourselves first because we surely spend more time, use more words, are affected more deeply in talking to ourselves than to others. Each of us is, to borrow a phrase from Wendell Johnson, "our own most enchanted listener." Perhaps Langer was right. Why do we talk to ourselves? Does it enhance our survival? What is so important that we are impelled to talk to ourselves so incessantly—indeed, not only when awake but when sleeping as well?

One answer that can provide schooling with a profound organizing principle is that we use language to create the world—which is to say, language is not only a vehicle of thought; it is, as Wittgenstein said, also the driver. We go where it leads. We see the world as it permits us to see it. There is, to be sure, a world of "not-words." But, unlike all the other creatures on the planet, we have access to it only through the world of words, which we ourselves have created and continue to create. Language allows us to name things, but, more than that, it also suggests what feelings we are obliged to associate with the things we name. Even more, language controls what things shall be named, what things we ought to pay attention to. Language even tells us what things are things. In English, "lightning" is a thing, and so is a "wave," and an "explosion." Even ideas are made to appear as things. English makes us believe, for example, that "time" is moving in a straight line from "yesterday" to "today" to "tomorrow." If we ask ourselves, Where did yesterday go? Where is tomorrow waiting?, we may get a sense of how much these words are ideas more than things and of how much the world as we imagine it is a product of how we describe it. There is no escaping the fact that when we form a sentence, we are creating a world. We are organizing it, making it pliable, understandable, useful. In the beginning, there was the word, and in the end, as well. Is anyone in our schools taking this seriously?

Perhaps Mrs. Soybel did, but thought we were too young to grasp the idea. If so, she was mistaken. There are many ways to teach the young the connections between language and world-making. But she made still another mistake, one common enough, by giving her students the impression that the important thing about language is to know the difference between "he don't" and "he doesn't," to spell "recommendation" correctly, and never to pronounce the name of our city, "Noo Yawk." Some might say that if she taught those lessons well, she did enough. But what, then, of the junior high teachers, the high school teachers, the college teachers? By failing to reveal the story of human beings as world-makers through language, they miss several profound opportunities. They fail, for example, to convey the idea that there is an inescapable moral dimension to how we use language. We are instructed in the Bible never to take the name of the Lord in vain. What other names must we never take in vain? And why? A fair answer is that language distinguishes between the sacred and the profane, and thereby provides organization to our moral sense. The profligate use of language is not merely a social offense but a threat to the ways in which we have constructed our notions of good and bad, permissible and impermissible. To use language to defend the indefensible (as George Orwell claimed some of us habitually do), to use language to transform certain human beings into nonpersons, to use language to lie and to blur distinctions, to say more than you know or *can* know, to take the name of the truth in vain—these are offenses against a moral order, and they can, incidentally, be committed with excellent pronunciation or with impeccable grammar and spelling. Our engagement with language almost always has a moral dimension, a point that has been emphasized by every great philosopher from Confucius and Socrates to Bertrand Russell and John Dewey. How is it possible that a teacher, at any level, could miss it?

Of course, language also has a social dimension. Mrs. Soybel understood this well enough, but only part of it. Her idea was that by abandoning homegrown dialects, her gaggle of Brooklyn ragamuffins could become linguistically indistinguishable from Oxford dons, or at least American corporate executives. What she may have missed is that in changing our speech, we would be changing our politics, our taste, our passions, our sense of beauty, even our loyalties. Perhaps she did know this, but the matter was never explained or discussed, and no choice was offered. Would such changes alienate us from our parents, relatives, and friends? Is there something wrong with being from the "working class"? What new prejudices will become comfortable and what old ones despicable? In seeing the world through the prism of new ways of speaking, would we be better or worse? These are questions of large import, and they need to be raised these days in the context of the effort to have us speak in "politically correct" ways. By changing our names for things, how do we become different? What new social attitudes do we embrace? How powerful are our habitual ways of naming?

These are matters that ought to be at the heart of education. They are not merely about how we sound to others but about how we are sounding out the world. Of course, they are no more important than how language controls the uses of our intellect—that is to say, how our ideas of ideas are governed by language. Aristotle believed he had uncovered universal laws of thought, when, in fact, all he had done was to explain the logical rules of Greek syntax. Perhaps if the Greeks had been interested in other languages, he would have come to different conclusions. The medieval churchmen thought that if their language contained a word, there must necessarily be something in the world to which it corresponded, which sent them on a fruitless intellectual journey to discover how many angels could dance on the head of a pin. The well-known German philosopher Martin Heidegger believed that only the German language could express the subtlest and most profound philosophical notions. Perhaps he meant incomprehensible notions. In any case, his claim is weakened by the fact that he was an ardent supporter of Adolf Hitler and a member of the Nazi party. Apparently, he was somewhat unclear about what constitutes subtlety and profundity. But to the extent to which any of us is clear about anything, it will be through an awareness of how we use language, how language uses us, and what measures are available to clarify our knowledge of the world we make.

All of this is part of the great story of how humans use language to transform the world and then, in turn, are transformed by their own invention. The story, of course, did not end with the invention of speech. In fact, it begins there, which is what Mrs. Soybel may have meant in saying speech made us human. The story continued to unfold with fantastic twists as human beings invented surrogate languages to widen their scope: ideographs, phonetic writing, then printing, then telegraphy, photography, radio, movies, television, and computers, each of which transformed the world—sliced it, framed it, enlarged it, diminished it. To say of all this that we are merely toolmakers is to miss the point of the story. We are the world makers, and the word weavers. That is what makes us smart, and dumb; moral and immoral; tolerant and bigoted. That is what makes us human. Is it possible to tell this story to our young in school, to have them investigate how we advance our humanity by controlling the codes with which we address the world, to have them learn what happens when we lose control of our own inventions? This may be the greatest story untold. In school.

PART II

What you have just read in Part I, to paraphrase a famous sage, is the doctrine; what follows in Part II is the commentary. But I hasten to say that I make no claim that the five narratives I have described exhaust the possibilities. They merely exhaust my imagination. That there are still more ideas that can provide respectable, humane, and substantive reasons for schooling, I have no doubt. The purpose of this book is not only to put forward reasons that make sense but to play a role in promoting a serious conversation *about* reasons. Not about policies, management, assessment, and other engineering matters. These are important, but they ought rightfully to be addressed *after* decisions are made about what schools are for. Meaning only slight disrespect to some of my colleagues, I have the impression that of all those who have business to conduct with schools—school administrators, classroom teachers, students, parents, politicians, publishers, and professors of education—it is the last who seem least interested in talking about reasons, with the first not far behind. Perhaps I am wrong about this, but, in any case, we cannot fail to improve the lives of our young if all parties could enter the conversation with enthusiasm and resolve.

Part II intends to make its contribution by providing levels of specificity to the narratives described in Part I. Without such specificity, the narratives may appear abstract, airy, and possibly impractical. In what follows, I wish to show that they are nothing of the sort.

5 · The Spaceship Earth

Having just remarked that the narratives described in the last chapter may appear abstract and that I intend here to bring them down to earth, I take a risk in beginning with a fable. What could be more abstract than that? The reader may help to ease my mind by remembering, first, that this is a fable and not a curriculum and, second, that you need not burden it or yourself with doubts about its practicality. There will be time for that in addressing the moral of the fable.

A Fable

Once upon a time in the city of New York, civilized life very nearly came to an end. The streets were covered with dirt, and there was no one to tidy them. The air and rivers were polluted, and no one could cleanse them. The schools were run-down, and no one believed in them. Each day brought a new strike, and each strike brought new hardships. Crime and strife and disorder and rudeness were to be found everywhere. The young fought the old. The workers fought the students. The poor fought the rich. The city was bankrupt.

When things came to their most desperate moment, the

city fathers met to consider the problem. But they could suggest no cures, for their morale was very low and their imaginations dulled by hatred and confusion. There was nothing for the mayor to do but to declare a state of emergency. He had done this before during snowstorms and power failures, but now he felt even more justified.

"Our city," he said, "is under siege, like the ancient cities of Jericho and Troy. But *our* enemies are sloth and poverty and indifference and hatred."

As you can see, he was a very wise mayor, but not so wise as to say exactly how these enemies could be dispersed. Thus, though a state of emergency officially existed, neither the mayor nor anyone else could think of anything to do that would make the situation better rather than worse. And then an extraordinary thing happened.

One of the mayor's aides, knowing full well what the future held for the city, had decided to flee with his family to the country. In order to prepare himself for his exodus to a strange environment, he began to read Henry David Thoreau's *Walden*, which he had been told was a useful handbook on how to survive in the country. While reading the book, he came upon the following passage: "Students should not play life, or study it merely, while the community supports them at this expensive game, but earnestly live it from beginning to end. How could youths better learn to live than by at once trying the experiment of living?"

The aide sensed immediately that he was in the presence of an exceedingly good idea. And he sought an audience with the mayor. He showed the passage to the mayor, who was extremely depressed and in no mood to read from books, since he had already scoured books of lore and wisdom in search of help but had found nothing.

"What does it mean?" asked the mayor angrily.

"Nothing less," replied the aide, "than a way to our salvation."

He then explained to the mayor that the students in the public schools had heretofore been part of the general problem, whereas, with some imagination and a change of perspective, they might easily become part of the general solution. He pointed out that from junior high school through senior high school, there were approximately 400,000 able-bodied, energetic young men and women who could be used as a resource to make the city livable again.

"But how can we use them?" asked the mayor. "And what would happen to their education if we did?"

To this, the aide replied, "They will find their education in the process of saving their city. And as for their lessons in school, we have ample evidence that the young do not exactly appreciate them and are even now turning against their teachers and their schools." The aide, who had come armed with statistics (as aides are wont to do), pointed out that the city was spending $1 million a year merely replacing broken school windows and that almost one-third of all the students enrolled in the schools did not show up on any given day.

"Yes, I know," said the mayor sadly. "Woe unto us."

"Wrong," said the aide brashly. "The boredom and destructiveness and pent-up energy that are an affliction to us can be turned to our advantage."

The mayor was not quite convinced, but having no better idea of his own, he appointed his aide chairman of the Emergency Education Committee, and the aide at once made plans to remove almost 400,000 students from their dreary classrooms and their even drearier lessons, so that their energy and talents might be used to repair the desecrated environment.

When these plans became known, there was a great hue

and cry against them, for people in distress will sometimes prefer a problem that is familiar to a solution that is not. For instance, the teachers complained that their contract contained no provision for such unusual procedures. To this, the aide replied that the *spirit* of their contract compelled them to help educate our youth, and that education can take many forms and be conducted in many places. "It is not written in any holy book," he observed, "that an education must occur in a small room with chairs in it."

Some parents complained that the plan was un-American and that its compulsory nature was hateful to them. To this, the aide replied that the plan was based on the practices of earlier Americans who required the young to assist in controlling the environment in order to ensure the survival of the group. "Our schools," he added, "have never hesitated to compel. The question is not, nor has it ever been, to compel or not to compel but, rather, which things ought to be compelled."

And even some children complained, although not many. They said that their God-given right to spend twelve years of their lives, at public expense, sitting in a classroom was being trampled. To this complaint, the aide replied that they were confusing a luxury with a right and that, in any case, the community could no longer afford either. "Besides," he added, "of all the God-given rights man has identified, none takes precedence over his right to survive."

And so, the curriculum of the public schools of New York City became known as Operation Survival, and all the children from seventh grade through twelfth grade became part of it. Here are some of the things they were obliged to do:

On Monday morning of every week, 400,000 children had to help clean up their own neighborhoods. They swept the streets, canned the garbage, removed the litter from empty lots, and hosed the dust and graffiti from the pavements and walls. Wednesday mornings were reserved for beautifying the city. Students planted trees and flowers, tended the grass and shrubs, painted subways and other eyesores, and even repaired broken-down public buildings, starting with their own schools.

Each day, five thousand students (mostly juniors and seniors in high school) were given responsibility to direct traffic on city streets, so that all the policemen who previously had done this were freed to keep a sharp eye out for criminals. Each day, five thousand students were asked to help deliver the mail, so that it soon became possible to have mail delivered twice a day—as it had been done in days of yore.

Several thousand students were also used to establish and maintain day-care centers, so that young mothers, many on welfare, were free to find gainful employment. Each student was also assigned to meet with two elementary school students on Tuesday and Thursday afternoons to teach them to read, to write, and to do arithmetic. Twenty thousand students were asked to substitute, on one afternoon a week, for certain adults whose jobs the students could perform without injury or loss of efficiency. These adults were then free to attend school or, if they preferred, to assist the students in their efforts to save their city.

The students were also assigned to publish a newspaper in every neighborhood of the city, and in it, they were able to include much information that good citizens need to have. Students organized science fairs, block parties, and rock festivals, and they formed, in every neighborhood, both an orchestra and a theater company. Some students assisted in hospitals, helped to register voters, and produced radio and television programs that were aired on city stations. There was still time to hold a year-round City Olympics, in which every child competed in some sport or other.

It came to pass, as you might expect, that the college students in the city yearned to participate in the general plan, and thus another 100,000 young people became available to serve the community. The college students ran a jitney service from the residential boroughs to Manhattan and back. Using their own cars and partly subsidized by the city, the students quickly established a kind of auxiliary, semipublic transportation system, which reduced the number of cars coming into Manhattan, took some of the load off the subways, and diminished air pollution—in one stroke.

College students were empowered to give parking and littering tickets, thus freeing policemen more than ever for real detective work. They were permitted to organize seminars, film festivals, and lectures for junior and senior high school students; and on a UHF television channel, set aside for the purpose, they gave advanced courses in a variety of subjects every day from 3:00 p.m. to 10:00 p.m. They also helped to organize and run drug-addiction rehabilitation centers, and they launched campaigns to inform people of their legal rights, nutritional needs, and available medical facilities.

Because this is a fable and not a fairy tale, it cannot be said that all the problems of the city were solved. But several extraordinary things did happen. The city began to come alive, and its citizens found new reason to hope that they could save themselves. Young people who had been alienated from their environment assumed a proprietary interest in it. Older people who had regarded the young as unruly and parasitic came to respect them. There followed from this a revival of courtesy and a diminution of crime, for there was less reason than before to be angry at one's neighbors and wish to assault them.

Amazingly, most of the students found that while they did not "receive" an education, they were able to create a quite adequate one. They lived, each day, their social studies and geography and communication and biology lessons and many other things that decent and proper people know about, including the belief that everyone must share equally in creating a livable city, no matter what he or she becomes later on. It even came to pass that the older people, being guided by the example of the young, took a renewed interest in restoring their environment and at the very least refused to participate in its destruction.

Now, it would be foolish to deny that there were not certain problems attending this whole adventure. For instance, thousands of children who would otherwise have known the principal rivers of Uruguay had to live out their lives in ignorance of these facts. Hundreds of teachers felt that their training had been wasted, because they could not educate children unless it were done in a classroom. As you can imagine, it was also exceedingly difficult to grade students on their activities, and after a while, almost all tests ceased. This made many people unhappy, for many reasons, but most of all because no one could tell the dumb children from the smart children anymore.

But the mayor, who was, after all, a very shrewd politician, promised that as soon as the emergency was over, everything would be restored to normal. Meanwhile, everybody lived happily ever after—in a state of emergency, but quite able to cope with it.

. . .

Those who have read or heard this fable (it has appeared twice in the *New York Times Magazine*), and were then asked to state its moral, have come up with at least six different ones. Whether this makes it a good fable or not, I do not know. But the moral I prefer is that a sense of responsibility for the planet is born from a sense of responsibility for one's own neighborhood. It is hard to imagine that anyone who fouls his or her own nest could care very much about the tree in which it is lodged. Thus, the fable suggests that we must begin the story of the Earth as our spaceship by inventing ways to engage students in the care of their own schools, neighborhoods, and towns. Those who claim to be in close touch with what they call "reality" point out that a proposal such as this one poses insurmountable problems in supervision and would require planning of such care that most schools or school systems would be defeated right at the start. They also observe that proposals of this kind have political and legal implications that go far beyond anything the schools have ever had to cope with. I reluctantly but emphatically agree. When one considers that most schools have difficulty in simply providing students with nutritious lunches, the specific activities described in the fable would seem to be a prescription for chaos. But there is an idea here that ought not to be easily dismissed. Yes, it is unrealistic to expect students to direct traffic or deliver the mail. But is it unrealistic to have them clean and paint their own school, plant trees and flowers, produce a community newspaper, create a community theater? Is it unrealistic for older students to teach younger ones? In fact, there are several schools that already allow, if they do not require, students to do such things, and to do them for the right reasons. I would stress the phrase "for the right reasons." There are, for example, many schools that have enthusiastically developed what are called "work

study" or "apprenticeship" programs with a view toward fa-
miliarizing the young with the world of work. It is not clear
to me why the schools are so interested in such an objective.[1]
Students will have most of their lives to familiarize themselves with the world of work—work is something they will
have to do. Caring for their environment is not something
they will have to do, and, one fears, most don't. The purpose
of the activities suggested by the fable is to introduce the
young to their responsibilities for the planet, beginning with
the buildings and streets that are their portion of the planet.
The idea is to show that the environment is not something
one is given, take it or leave it. The fact is that we cannot leave
it, and neither should we take it. Rather, we must make it.
And to make it requires a consciousness of our interdependence, as well as an encouragement and legitimization of the
effort.

I should add that among the "new" ideas now current in
several places is the organization of schooling around
themes. This is a progressive idea, pointing as it does to the
need for providing meaning in education. It also explicitly rejects the common assumption that the subjects of a curriculum have nothing to do with one another. But there are trivial
themes, and idiotic themes, and themes that are trendy but, in
the end, explain nothing and lead nowhere. The spaceship
Earth is not, I believe, among these. We may think of it as the
"negentropic" theme, which includes the idea that the test of
a civilization, as Eric Hoffer has reminded us, is in its capacity for maintenance. To build a house is a fine and noble thing,
but to keep it from crumbling is the essential task of a civilization. That the young are not exempt from this task is the
message of this theme.

But that message implies still another—that we cannot afford to waste the energy and potential idealism of the young.

There is no question that listlessness, ennui, and even violence in school are related to the fact that students have no useful role to play in society. The strict application of nurturing and protective attitudes toward children has created a paradoxical situation in which protection has come to mean excluding the young from meaningful involvement in their own communities. It is hardly utopian to try to invent forms of youthful participation in social reconstruction as an alternative or supplement to the schooling process. Moreover, as things stand now in many places, the energy of the young works in opposition to learning; that is, it is an *obstacle* that schooling must overcome. What I am proposing intends to use youthful energy as an asset to students' academic experience. This is the principle of "Judo," in which one uses the strength of one's opponent as an addition to one's own strength. In this case, we do not suppress the energy of students; rather, we exploit it for benign, constructive, and humane purposes.

For those realists who think the fable and its implications are impractical, I now propose another idea that would appear to be more conventional but is probably more "impractical." In this one, the students stay in school, take academic subjects, and can even be tested or, as realists like to say, have their learning assessed. I propose that we realign the structure of what are called "major subjects" so that (if you will forgive an unplanned alliteration) archaeology, anthropology, and astronomy are given the highest priority. What makes this "impractical" is the fact that subjects are, as much as anything else, bureaucratic and institutional entities. Teachers are licensed by the state to teach a subject; publishers produce textbooks in subjects; national organizations are formed around subjects. To turn a "major" subject into a "minor" one, or to eliminate a subject altogether, or to introduce a new one is a significant legal and political matter and is bound to arouse opposition. Nonetheless, the matter is worth serious consideration, all the more so because there is, after all, a measure of arbitrariness to the weight given to one subject or another. When I attended public school (in New York City), both music and art were considered "minor" subjects—for what reason, I have no idea. There was then a High School of Music and Art (and still is), so that someone must have thought these subjects were of sufficient import to organize learning around them. But not in my schools. Even further, geography was treated as a separate subject, and, if my memory serves accurately, so was public speaking. Neither makes the grade in most schools now. Of course, these days, computer science and media studies are regarded as subjects (in New Mexico, media studies is required in high school), and I know of more than one high school that gives courses in such subjects as sports writing. In other words, for all the seeming solidity of the subjects in a curriculum, changes do take place, and usually for reasons that may be said to be "educational."

In this context, it would be helpful if the training of teachers and administrators included attention to the history of "subjects" so that there might be some understanding of how, when, and why subjects were formed. This would assist in shielding school people from the dangers of hardening of the categories. "English," for example, was not a subject in American schools until the 1920s. The ancient Greeks had a curriculum formed around the study of "harmonics," and so lumped together (as major subjects) arithmetic, astronomy, music, and geometry. The Sophists taught grammar, logic, and rhetoric, the last two of which have little importance in American schools. I wonder why. (Plato thought logic shouldn't be studied until one reached the age of thirty-five. But I don't think that is the reason we mostly ignore it.) The

Greeks, by the way, had no interest in or respect for any language but their own and would have thought courses in "foreign languages" an absurdity. My favorite subject of all time is found in the curriculum developed by Confucius, which required students to study and practice archery—not, incidentally, because they were being trained as warriors, but because the subject taught them discipline, precision, and concentration. Confucius also insisted on students' studying what we would call "good manners." Can you imagine a school today requiring as a major subject the study and practice of good manners? Surely, no one can say it is not an important subject. Perhaps it is not in the curriculum because the Educational Testing Service would be hard-pressed to figure out how to assess it.

Why then archaeology? The argument is strong, although I should say at once I do not have in mind the study of how archaeologists do their work. There are interesting possibilities in allowing the young to learn something about the methods of archaeologists, but I am content to let that part of the subject reside in graduate school. I am referring here to the knowledge that archaeologists have produced about what is sometimes called "prehistory." If we are interested in increasing awareness of the preciousness of the Earth, of its place as our home, both in the past and the future, then no subject will serve as well as archaeology. There was a time when students were given, once over lightly, some knowledge of the great achievements of ancient Egyptian civilization. In those days, "Tigris and Euphrates" was the answer to at least one test question, and the phrase "the cradle of civilization" was not entirely unknown to sixth graders. But the matter was never pursued with much conviction, and is rarely done so today. This was, and is, a serious mistake, especially in light of the knowledge acquired in this century about humanity's "recent" past. We know, for example, that the Sumerians were writing on clay tablets at least a thousand years before Abraham departed from the land of Ur, and epic poetry was being written by the Babylonians a thousand years before Moses is supposed to have taken the Ten Commandments down from Mount Sinai. We know that the Bible, commonly regarded as the book on which Western morality and social organization are founded, took many of its themes from the great Babylonian epic, *Gilgamesh*. The first great Chinese dictionary, containing forty thousand characters, was compiled 3,500 years ago (the first great English dictionary, 200 years ago). The Sumerians were writing in cuneiform fifteen hundred years before the alphabet was invented, and three thousand years ago, the Chinese used a math textbook that included root multiplications, geometry, and equations with more than one unknown quantity.

The Sumerians, I might add, provided us with the first documented—that is, written—record of schools, of proverbs and sayings, of love songs, of library catalogues, of resurrection tales, of legal precedent, and of tax reduction. That is to say, in studying the ancients, whether Sumerian, Babylonian, Egyptian, or Chinese, we are not only studying civilizations but *people*. They lived on Earth, complained, grieved, rejoiced, cheated one another, scolded their children, fell in battle, wrote poetry, and did many other things that people from Kansas City do this very day. It does them no discredit that they could not imagine using e-mail or watching television. Neither are they to be taken lightly because they did not know about the universe or the Milky Way or even the solar system. But they knew something about the Earth and how to take care of it, and what happens when its care is a matter of indifference.

Archaeology, then, is among the best subjects we have for

helping to cultivate in the young a sense of earthly perspective. Crew members of the spaceship Earth need to have nontrivial knowledge of crew members of the past. After all, they will be the Sumerians three thousand years from now, and their accomplishments and ignorances will be the subject of review by crew members of the future. Some sense of the continuity of humanity's sojourn on Earth would seem a necessity.

There are two more points that need to be made here about archaeology, which is normally regarded as an arcane subject. First, instruction in it ought to begin at an early age, and continue in spiraling levels of complexity and sophistication through college. I do not say I know exactly how this might be done with, say, fifth graders, never having had a chance to try it. I began my career as a fifth-grade teacher, and was told (this was many years ago) that there was no time for such a subject, especially because it was not "basic." I have no objection to schools' confining their instruction to what is basic. The question, of course, is exactly that: What is basic? Or, to put it better, What are the subjects that are suited to provide students with meaning? Prehistory, it seems to me, is one such subject, and I have no doubt that good elementary teachers can figure out how to introduce and pursue the subject.

Second, in pursuing the subject, teachers must not only have substantive knowledge but are required to exercise extreme tact. There are many students who come to school bound to cosmological narratives that contradict archaeological scholarship. For example, not long ago I had two students (undergraduates) who believed that the Earth was created at 9:00 a.m. on October 23, 4004 B.C. Their story had no place in it for claims that took human life further back than that. One approach—which, I fear, did not work—was for me to explain that significant learning often produces confusion and even sadness, since knowledge does not always give support to cherished beliefs. I even quoted from Ecclesiastes (1:18) to provide some comfort: "For in much wisdom is much grief; and he that increaseth knowledge increaseth sorrow." They were not as impressed as I am with the insights of the Preacher.

An alternative approach is to present archaeology as a narrative (which it is) and not as a definitive, ultimate truth rendering all competing narratives null and void. Educators may bring upon themselves unnecessary travail by taking a tactless and unjustifiable position about the relation between scientific and religious narratives. We see this, of course, in the conflict concerning creation science. Some educators representing, as they think, the conscience of science act much like those legislators who in 1925 prohibited by law the teaching of evolution in Tennessee. In that case, anti-evolutionists were fearful that a scientific idea would undermine religious belief. Today, pro-evolutionists are fearful that a religious idea will undermine scientific belief. The former had insufficient confidence in religion; the latter insufficient confidence in science. The point is that profound but contradictory ideas may exist side by side, if they are constructed from different materials and methods and have different purposes. Each tells us something important about where we stand in the universe, and it is foolish to insist that they must despise each other. There are two relevant quotations that make this point, each from a man who had more than a passing interest in the matter. The first is from none other than Galileo, who in urging that a distinction be made between religious and scientific narratives remarked that "the intention of the Holy Spirit is to teach how one goes to heaven, not how heaven goes." The second, coming 375 years later, is from Pope John Paul II: "Science can purify religion from error and superstition. Religion can purify science from idolatry and false absolutes."[2]

It is here that the subject of anthropology comes in, since, unlike archaeology, it presents to us living cultures that differ widely in their worldviews and therefore helps the young to defend themselves against idolatry and false absolutes. With some reservations previously noted, I call upon the *Enterprise* (from *Star Trek*) as a useful metaphor of what an anthropological outlook may teach. Like our planet itself, the *Enterprise* is home to a variety of groups, not all of them Earth people. Spock, for example, is half Vulcan, and from time to time Romulans and even the fearsome Klingons will share space with the Earth people. Of course, they have their own spaceships, but if we can imagine (for reasons Gene Roddenberry might have thought of) that all of them had to live on the *Enterprise*, we would have a fairly accurate picture of what our situation is: a community of different languages, different traditions, different physiques (and therefore different standards of beauty), and different cosmological narratives. The following questions would arise: What does each group have to know about the others? What knowledge would lead to harmony? What knowledge might lead to conflict? On what basis would any group claim superiority over the others? Would it be possible to create a narrative, including a set of symbols, that would attract the allegiance of all groups?

Questions like these are relevant to a consideration of what students need to know not only about Eskimo, Hopi, and Brazilian rain-forest people but about Iranians, Vietnamese, Finns, Canadians, and all the others with whom they share the spaceship. There is, of course, a clear ideological bias to anthropology, as there is to the theme of the spaceship Earth—that ignorance, distrust, and intolerance of difference are

dangers to the spaceship and that anything that might be done
to reduce them helps to ensure everyone's survival. But I must
add at once that such an outlook does not necessarily lead to
an uncritical relativism. The Vulcans, as we know, take a
rather bemused attitude toward the Earthlings' excessive
emotionalism. The Earthlings, for their part, are quite sure that
the Vulcans place too much value on logic and calculation.
Each learns something from the other, which allows a measure
of harmony, even affection, to exist between them. But each retains the belief in the essential correctness of its worldview.
One does not have to be a cultural relativist in order to be tolerant of other views, at least not when survival is at stake. The
Klingons would present a special problem, since their culture
is organized around a distrustful belligerence. How the Earthlings, the Vulcans, and others would cope with the Klingons
is, of course, an exact analogy to a problem we have on our
own spaceship. The solution does not require that others accept the values of the Klingons, or that they regard that value
as being as good as any other. The solution requires, first, that
we recognize its existence; second, that we examine ourselves
to see how much we are like Klingons; and third, that we try
to find in Klingon culture elements of which we wholeheart-
edly approve. One probably should resist taking the *Enterprise*
as metaphor too far, but it is worth noting that in *Star Trek: The
Next Generation*, the Klingons and the Earthlings have become
friends and seem to worry about how to civilize the Romulans. Does this remind us of how America and "the evil Empire" have now joined their destinies and are trying to find
recognizable and admirable values in each other's culture?

Anthropology is clearly a subject of global dimensions,
and its early introduction to our young and its continued
study throughout schooling would help to give them an awe-
inspiring sense of humanity's range of difference, as well as a

sense of our common points. In learning about difference, we become less afraid and therefore more courageous. In learning about commonalities, we become more hopeful. Is there anything that our spaceship needs more than that its crew be courageous and hopeful?

But for a sense of awe, there is nothing to match astronomy. Happily, unlike archaeology and anthropology, astronomy is no stranger to school curriculums. I remember being taught (as part of general science—none of it general and some of it not science) about the planets, stars, and comets. I even recall looking at Vincent Dinato's paper during a test because I could not remember Neptune for the question requiring us to name all the planets. This was a fruitless effort at cheating, since Vincent only had Mars, Venus, and Earth as his answer, and it ended with Vincent looking at my paper. If only I had been sitting next to Mildred Waldman, both I *and* Vincent would have had perfect answers. But in studying astronomy fifty years ago, even the best students could not learn much more than Galileo, Tycho Brahe, and Kepler knew. There was a vague reference to a Big Bang theory but no evidence of it. No one knew anything about black holes. No one had been to the moon, and no satellite had visited Mars. No one had ever seen what the Earth looks like from a point outside the Earth. And we even believed that the solar system, having once been formed, would more or less always be exactly the same. I am writing in the year when twenty-one pieces of the Shoemaker-Levy 9 comet, traveling at unimaginable speeds, crashed into Jupiter, enabling us to see for ourselves that the solar system is not a fixed thing, but an ongoing process. It changed, as it were, before our very eyes. Naturally, and humanly, our astonishment was accompanied by worry about what might happen to our own spaceship if it were assaulted by a comet. Everyone agreed that were a comet to visit us, the differences between Iranians and Germans, Canadians and Finns, would melt away as quickly and decisively as would portions of the planet.

Astronomy is, of course, the subject that most explicitly depicts our planet as a spaceship, and its study inevitably raises fundamental questions about ourselves and our mission. Are we, for example, alone in the universe? In surveying the multitude of galaxies, Thomas Carlyle addressed the question with a sullen comment. "A sad spectacle," he remarked. "If they be inhabited, what a scope for misery and folly. If they not be inhabited, what a waste of space." But most young people are inspired rather than depressed by the vastness of the universe and the possibility of life on other spaceships. The fascination with space takes different forms, of course. The young ones may find excitement in imagining through art what the crews of other spaceships would look like. Older students, if they have some rudimentary physics, may enjoy speculating on how Earthlings might communicate with the crews in other parts of our galaxy. There may even be students who will find spiritual meaning in the fact that our ship and all that is on it appear to be at one with the universe. As far as we can tell, everything in the universe is made of the same stuff and follows the same rules. Thus, astronomy offers confirmation of an intuitive idea expressed over centuries by people of different cultures. Heraclitus wrote that all things are one. Lao-tzu said all things are ruled by a single principle. The Suquamish Indian chief Seattle declared that all things are connected. So it would seem. Even those who are believers in creation theory may find it encouraging that the Big Bang theory of modern astronomers is not so far from the story of the Beginning as found in Genesis. The thought that a group of camel-riding Bedouins huddling around a fire in the desert night four thousand years ago might ponder the question of how the universe began and come up with a narrative that is similar to one accepted by MIT professors in the late twentieth century speaks of a continuity of human imagination that cannot fail to inspire. That is not to say that in teaching astronomy, one must distort what is known in order to accommodate other narratives (although one might help Creationists to accommodate *their* story to astronomy). We know, for example, something about *how* our spaceship was created. We know *when* our spaceship was created—about 5 billion years ago. We know *where* we are in the universe—on a planet orbiting a star that is situated at the edge of a spiral galaxy, which is near the outskirts of a supercluster of galaxies. Of course, we do not know what we are here *for,* which is a question astronomy provokes but declines to address. Indeed, most astronomers are likely to agree that asking the question doesn't make any sense. They will refer us to other narratives if we wish to discuss it. But astronomers will agree that since we *are* here, and know that we are here, we have important responsibilities to our planet, such as not destroying our atmosphere or depleting the available oxygen or polluting the oceans. They will agree that human greed, ignorance, and indifference are a greater threat to the planet than comets.

Astronomy, then, is a key subject if we wish to cultivate in our young a sense of awe, interdependence, and global responsibility. But here something must be said about how the subject ought to be taught—in a word, historically. Every subject has a history, and as I will try to show in the next chapter, there is no better way to reveal how humans have overcome their mistakes than by tracking the history of subjects. But astronomy is especially well suited to an historical treatment because the record of its mistakes and corrections is so well documented. We know what Aristotle believed, what

Ptolemy believed, what Copernicus believed, and what Galileo believed. We even know the price some of them paid for their beliefs. Giordano Bruno said that God "is glorified not in one but in countless suns; not in a single earth but in a thousand, I say, in an infinity of worlds." For this belief, which, unlike Galileo, he did not recant, he was burned alive on February 19, 1600, even though fifteen hundred years before that, Lucretius expressed the same idea, and five hundred years before that, Metrodorus said the same.

The point is that astronomy is a human story, filled with the same emotions, drama, triumphs, and tragedies one finds in Shakespeare's plays. There is ambition, greed, deceit, superstition, nobility, wonder, and, always and above all else, curiosity. One may properly call astronomy science, but when taught as a struggle to discover where our spaceship is and how it comes to be there, we may also say the subject is one of the humanities. We may take as a guide here remarks made by William James on what constitutes a humanistic subject. He said: "You can give humanistic value to almost anything by teaching it historically. Geology, economics, mechanics, are humanities when taught with reference to the successive achievements of the geniuses to which these sciences owe their being. Not taught thus, literature remains grammar, art a catalogue, history a list of dates, and natural science a sheet of formulas and weights and measures."[3] To which I might add, not taught thus, astronomy becomes names of objects, which provokes nervous students to cheat on examinations.

In bringing this chapter to a close, I must also say that the teaching of foreign languages (so that students can actually speak one) and the study of comparative religion are indispensable means of enhancing the story of the spaceship Earth. But since I will discuss these in detail in chapters to follow, I am content here merely to note their importance.

6 · The Fallen Angel

I am not sure who said it (possibly Northrop Frye), but it has been remarked that there are three characters from literature who are known all over the world: Hamlet, Alice, and Sherlock Holmes. I don't know how Shakespeare and Lewis Carroll felt about their creations, but it is known that Arthur Conan Doyle believed Holmes to be something of a nuisance and thought that his stories about Holmes did not represent his best work. The irony, of course, is that no one reads what Doyle regarded as his best work, but everybody reads about Holmes.

Something like this will happen, on occasion, to lesser—much lesser—authors—for example, me. Among the many pages I have written about education over the years, I have included a few ideas that seemed to me to rise above the others, and could be expected to be given special consideration by readers. But the ideas have been largely ignored, mostly on the grounds that readers believed they were included as an attempt at humor. This is depressing for two reasons: first, that readers believed my sense of humor was so uninspired; second, that *their* sense of possibilities was so limited. You may judge for yourself. Here is one of the ideas. We could improve the quality of teaching overnight, as it were, if math teachers were assigned to teach art, art teachers science, science teachers English. My reasoning is as follows: Most teachers, especially high school and college teachers, teach subjects they were good at in school. They found the subject both easy and pleasurable. As a result, they are not likely to understand how the subject appears to those who are *not* good at it, or don't care about it, or both. If, let us say, for a semester, each teacher were assigned a subject which he or she hated or always had trouble with, the teacher would be forced to see the situation as most students do, would see things more as a new learner than as an old teacher. Perhaps he or she would discover how boring the textbooks are, would learn how nerve-racking the fear of making mistakes is, might discover that a question that has unsuspectingly aroused his or her interest must be ignored because it is not covered by the syllabus, might even discover that there are students who know the subject better than he or she could ever hope to. Then what?

All in all, I believe the experience would be chastening and even eye-opening. When teachers returned to their specialties, it is possible they would bring with them refreshing ideas about how to communicate about their subject, and with an increased empathy for their students.

Here is another idea, not meant to be funny: We can improve the quality of teaching and learning overnight by getting rid of all textbooks. Most textbooks are badly written and, therefore, give the impression that the subject is boring. Most textbooks are also impersonally written. They have no "voice," reveal no human personality. Their relationship to the reader is not unlike the telephone message that says, "If you want further assistance, press two now." I have found the recipes on the backs of cereal boxes to be written with more style and conviction than most textbook descriptions of the causes of the Civil War. Of the language of grammar texts, I will not even speak. To borrow from Shakespeare, it is unfit for a Christian ear to endure. But worse than this, textbooks are concerned with presenting the facts of the case (whatever the case may be) as if there can be no disputing them, as if they are fixed and immutable. And still worse, there is usually no clue given as to who claimed these are the facts of the case, or how "it" discovered these facts (there being no he or she, or I or we). There is no sense of the frailty or ambiguity of human judgment, no hint of the possibilities of error. Knowledge is presented as a commodity to be acquired, never as a human struggle to understand, to overcome falsity, to stumble toward the truth.

Textbooks, it seems to me, are enemies of education, instruments for promoting dogmatism and trivial learning. They may save the teacher some trouble, but the trouble they inflict on the minds of students is a blight and a curse.

On one occasion when I made this argument before a group of teachers, one of them asked, "But if we eliminated textbooks, what would replace them?" My answer—again, not meant humorously—was as follows: "When Jonas Salk's vaccine eliminated polio, did anyone ask, But what will replace it?" You might think I was being a wise guy, and so I was. The teacher deserved a better answer, and I will come to one. But first, I will offer one other idea that has been widely and consistently ignored. This one, I confess, was originated inadvertently by Reed Irvine, who heads a right-wing group called Accuracy in Media (AIM). The group's purpose is to monitor newspapers, radio, and television in a search for left-wing bias, which, when found, is to be exposed and condemned. A few years ago, Mr. Irvine began to extend his surveillances by forming a group known as Accuracy in Academia (AIA), whose purpose is to expose left-wing bias in the classroom. The idea is to have students secretly and carefully monitor the lectures and remarks of their teachers so that the latter's inaccuracies, clichés, and unjustified opinions may be brought to light. It is probably not entirely irrelevant to note that those of a "liberal" bent reacted with disdain, chagrin, and righteousness to the thought of student spies evaluating everything their teachers say. Perhaps it was the secrecy of it all that disturbed them. I hope so, because putting the secrecy aside, Accuracy in Academia is about the best idea yet invented for achieving what every teacher longs for: first, to get students to pay careful attention; second, to get them to think critically. Of course, the flaw in Irvine's idea is that he wishes students to think critically in only one direction. But this is easily corrected. All that is necessary is that at the beginning of each course, the teacher address students in the following way:

During this term, I will be doing a great deal of talking. I will be giving lectures, answering questions, and conducting discussions. Since I am an imperfect scholar and, even more certainly, a fallible human being, I will inevitably be making factual errors, drawing some unjustifiable conclusions, and perhaps passing along my opinions as facts. I should be very unhappy if you were unaware of these mistakes. To minimize that possibility, I am going to make you all honorary members of Accuracy in Academia. Your task is to make sure that none of my errors goes by unnoticed. At the beginning of each class, I will, in fact, ask you to reveal whatever errors I made in the previous session. You must, of course, say *why* these are errors, indicate the source of your authority, and, if possible, suggest a truer or more useful or less biased way of formulating what I said. Your grade in this course will be based to some extent on the rigor with which you pursue my mistakes.

And to ensure that you do not fall into the torpor that is so common among students, I will, from time to time, deliberately include some patently untrue statements and some outrageous opinions.

There is no need for you to do this alone. You should consult with your classmates, perhaps even form a study group that can collectively review the things I have said. Nothing would please me more than for one or several of you to ask for class time in which to present a corrected or alternative version of one of my lectures.

I am banking on readers' agreeing that these three ideas are neither humorous nor impractical. Neither do I see them as gimmicks. To try to renew a teacher's sense of the difference between teaching and learning, to eliminate packaged truths from the classroom, and to focus student attention on error are part of an uncommon but, I believe, profound narrative capable of generating interest and inspiration in school. It is, in fact, a refutation of a story that infuses so much of schooling as we know it and have known it for so long. I am referring to the story that says the following in a hundred ways to students: You come to school to learn important facts and enduring truths. Your teacher knows many of these, your textbooks still others. It is not your business to know where they came from or how. It would, in any case, be a waste of valuable time to burden you with the mistakes of those who *thought* they had discovered important facts and enduring truths. School is not a place for documenting error, but for revealing the true state of affairs.

Do I exaggerate? I don't think so. The sentences above, with some variations and a few addenda, express the attitude of most schools toward knowledge (especially, by the way, most colleges) and explain why a course or two in "critical thinking" is quite irrelevant. They also explain the easy appeal of the previously mentioned "cultural literacy" project developed by E. D. Hirsch, Jr. The idea there is for students to become acquainted with a thousand facts without pausing to know whose facts they are, how we come to know them, why they are deemed important and by whom. This leads quite directly to the state of mind sometimes called "justification-ism." As used, for example, by Henry Perkinson in *The Possibilities of Error*, the word refers to the tendency of most people to engage in a rigorous and "natural" defense of their own beliefs, not so much to explain their beliefs as to justify them. Although we are all accustomed to such performances, is there not something strange about this—this idea of education in which everyone is encouraged to justify, fight for, and defend what they believe, as if we did not know that our beliefs are flawed, imperfect, badly in need of improvement? It would take a satirist of Swiftian talent to show, first, how unseemly it is and then how deeply it offends the way people learn. I risk contradicting John Dewey's most famous aphorism by saying that though we may learn by doing, we learn far more by failing—by trial and error, by making mistakes, correcting them, making more mistakes, correcting them, and so on. We are all in need of remedial work, all the time. And this includes teachers, students, and textbooks. Can you imagine a school organized around this principle—that whatever ideas we have, we are in some sense wrong? We may have insufficient facts to support an idea; or some of the facts we have may be incorrect, perhaps generated by a festering emotion; or the conclusions we have drawn may not be entirely logical; or some definition we are employing may not be applicable; or we may be merely repeating an idea we have heard expressed by some authority and have not examined its implications carefully. Can you imagine schools whose epistemological story does not aim at producing a flotilla of fanatics, but, rather, people who proceed to learn with full consciousness of their own fallibility, as well as the fallibility of others?

How could such schools be created? Any plan would, of necessity, have its origin in a new way of educating teachers, because it would require a refocusing of the purpose of teaching. As things stand now, teachers are apt to think of themselves as truth tellers who hope to extend the intelligence of students by revealing to them, or having them discover, incontrovertible truths and enduring ideas. I would suggest a different metaphor: teachers as error detectors who hope to extend the intelligence of students by helping them reduce the mistakes in their knowledge and skills. In this way, if I may put it crudely, teachers become less interested in making students smart, more interested in making students less dumb. This is not a question of semantics. Or, if it is, it is not "mere" semantics. It is, in fact, the point of view taken by those who practice medicine and law. Physicians do, of course, have a conception of what is good health, but their *expertise* resides in their ability to identify ill health and to provide remedies for it. That is why, upon being consulted, their first and most important question is, What's wrong?

The same may be said of lawyers, whose expertise resides in their ability to identify injustice and to pursue methods to eliminate it. In fact, to be realistic about the matter, for most physicians, good health is defined as the absence of illness; for most lawyers, justice is defined as the absence of injustice. Physicians and lawyers, we might say, function as painkillers. The good ones know how to relieve us of illness and injustice. I am suggesting the role of painkiller for teachers whose purpose would be to relieve students of the burdens of error—in their facts, their inferences, their opinions, their skills, their prejudices.

It would not be easy to educate teachers to approach matters in this way. Unlike the study of sickness and injustice, the study of error has rarely been pursued in a systematic way. But this does not mean that the subject has no history. There are many honorable books that take human error as a theme. The early dialogues of Plato are little else but meditations on error. Acknowledging that he did not know what truth is, Socrates spent his time exposing the false beliefs of those who thought they did. Erasmus's *In Praise of Folly* also comes to mind, as does Jonathan Swift's *Gulliver's Travels*. In a more modern vein, one thinks of Jacques Ellul's *A Critique of the New Commonplaces*, Stephen Jay Gould's *The Mismeasure of Man*, I. A. Richards's *Practical Criticism*, Mina Shaughnessy's *Errors and Expectations*, and S. I. Hayakawa's *Language in Thought and Action*.

Such books are not normally included as part of the education of teachers. Were they to be used, teachers would be likely to come to three powerful conclusions. The first is that everyone makes errors, including those who write about error. None of us is ever free of it, and we are most seriously endangered when we think we are. That there is an almost infinite supply of error, including our own, should provide teachers with a sense of humility and, incidentally, assurance that they will never become obsolete.

The second conclusion is that error is reducible. At present, teachers consume valuable time in pointless debates over whether or not intelligence is fixed, whether it is mostly genetic or environmental, what kinds of intelligences exist, and even how much intelligence one or another different race has. Such debates about error are entirely unnecessary. Error is a form of behavior. It is not something we *have;* it is something we *do*. Unlike intelligence, it is neither a metaphor nor a hypothetical construct whose presence is inferred by a score on a test. We can see error, read it, hear it. And it is possible to reduce its presence.

The third conclusion is that error is mostly committed with the larynx, tongue, lips, and teeth—which is to say, error is chiefly embodied in talk. It is true enough that our ways of talking are controlled by the ways we manage our minds, and no one is quite sure what "mind" is. But we *are* sure that the main expression of mind is sentences. When we are thinking, we are mostly arranging sentences in our heads. When we are making errors, we are arranging erroneous sentences. Even when we make a nonverbal error, we have preceded the action by talking to ourselves in such a way as to make us think the act is correct. The word, in a word, brings forth the act. This fact provides teachers with a specific subject matter in which they may become "experts": Their expertise would reside in their knowledge of those ways of talking that lead to unnecessary mischief, failure, misunderstanding, and even pain.

I believe Bertrand Russell had something like this in mind when he said that the purpose of education is to help students defend themselves against "the seductions of eloquence," their own "eloquence" as well as that of others. As I have previously mentioned, the ancient Greeks—that is, the Sophists—believed that the study of grammar, logic, and rhetoric would provide an adequate defense. These arts of language were assumed to be what may be called "metasubjects," subjects about subjects. Their rules, guidelines, principles, and insights were thought to be useful in thinking about *anything*.

In poking fun at those who saw no purpose in learning about language, Erasmus (in his *In Praise of Folly*) wrote with sharp irony: ". . . what use of grammar, where every man spoke the same language and had no further design than to understand one another? What use of logic, where there was no bickering about the double-meaning words? What need of rhetoric, where there were no lawsuits?"

He meant to say that as humans we will always have difficulty understanding one another, will always bicker about the meaning of words, always claim we have been injured by another. There is nothing that happens among humans that is not instigated, negotiated, clarified, or mystified by language, including our attempts to acquire knowledge. The Greeks, and, indeed, the medieval Schoolmen, understood well something we seem to have forgotten—namely, that all subjects are forms of discourse and that therefore almost all education is a form of language education. Knowledge of a subject mostly means knowledge of the language of that subject. Biology, after all, is not plants and animals; it is a special language employed to speak about plants and animals. History is not events that once occurred; it is language describing and interpreting events, according to rules established by historians. Astronomy is not planets and stars but a special way of talking about planets and stars, quite different from the language poets use to talk about them.

And so a student must know the language of a subject, but that is only the beginning. For it is not sufficient to know the definition of a noun, or a gene, or a molecule. One must also know what a definition is. It is not sufficient to know the right answers. One must also know the questions that produced them. Indeed, one must also know what a question is, for not every sentence that ends with a rising intonation or begins with an interrogative is necessarily a question. There are sentences that look like questions but cannot generate any meaningful answers, and, as Francis Bacon said, if they linger in our minds, they become obstructions to clear thinking. One must also know what a metaphor is, and what is the relationship between words and the things they describe. In short, one must have some knowledge of a metalanguage—a language about language—to recognize error, to defend oneself against the seductions of eloquence.

In a later chapter, I will offer a more detailed description of what such a metalanguage might consist of for modern students. Here, I should like to suggest some other means of educating students to be error detectors—for example, that all subjects be taught from an historical perspective. I can think of no better way to demonstrate that knowledge is not a fixed thing but a continuous struggle to overcome prejudice, authoritarianism, and even "common sense." Every subject, of course, has a history, including physics, mathematics, biology, and history itself. I have previously quoted William James to the effect that any subject becomes "humanistic" when taught historically. His point almost certainly was that there is nothing more human than the stories of our errors and how we have managed to overcome them, and then fallen into error again, and continued our efforts to make corrections—stories without end. Robert Maynard Hutchins referred to these stories as the Great Conversation, a dynamic and accurate metaphor, since it suggests not only that knowledge is passed down from one thinker to another but modified, refined, and corrected as the "conversation" goes on.

To teach about the atom without including Democritus in the conversation, electricity without Faraday, political science without Aristotle or Machiavelli, astronomy without Ptolemy, is to deny our students access to the Great Conversation. "To remain ignorant of things that happened before you were born is to remain a child," Cicero said. He then added, "What is a human life worth unless it is incorporated into the lives of one's ancestors and set in an historical context?" When we incorporate the lives of our ancestors in our education, we discover that some of them were great error-makers, some great error-correctors, some both. And in discovering this, we accomplish three things. First, we help students to see that knowledge is a stage in human development, with a past and a future. Second (this would surely please Professor E. D. Hirsch, Jr.), we acquaint students with the people and ideas that comprise "cultural literacy"—that is to say, give them some understanding of where their ideas come from and how we came by them. And third, we show them that error is no disgrace, that it is the agency through which we increase understanding.

Of course, to ensure that the last of these lessons be believed, we would have to make changes in what is called "the classroom environment." At present, there is very little tolerance for error in the classroom. That is one of the reasons students cheat. It is one of the reasons students are nervous. It is one of the reasons many students are reluctant to speak. It is certainly the reason why students (and the rest of us) fight so hard to justify what they think they know. In varying degrees, being wrong is a disgrace; one pays a heavy price for it. But suppose students found themselves in a place where this was not the case? In his book *Mindstorms*, Seymour Papert contends that one of the best reasons for using computers in the classroom is that computers *force* the environment to be more tolerant of error. Students move toward the right answer (at least in mathematics) by making mistakes and then correcting them. The computer does not humiliate students for being wrong, and it encourages them to try again. If Papert is right, then we do, indeed, have a good reason for having students use computers. Of course, if he is right, it is also an insult to teachers. Is it only through the introduction of a machine that the classroom can become a place where trial and error is an acceptable mode of learning, where being wrong is not a punishable offense?

Suppose teachers made it clear that all the materials introduced in class were not to be regarded as authoritative and final but, in fact, as problematic—textbooks, for example. (And here is my more serious answer to the teacher who wondered what we would do without them.) It is best, of course, to eliminate them altogether, replacing them with documents and other materials carefully selected by the individual teacher (what else is the Xerox machine for?). But if elimination is too traumatic, then we would not have to do without them, only without their customary purpose. We would start with the premise that a textbook is a particular person's attempt to explain something to us, and thereby tell us the truth of some matter. But we would know that this person could not be telling us the whole truth. Because no one can. We would know that this person has certain prejudices and biases. Because everyone has. We would know that this person must have included some disputable facts, shaky opinions, and faulty conclusions. Thus, we have good reason to use this person's textbook as an object of inquiry. What might have been left out? What are the prejudices? What are the disputable facts, opinions, and conclusions? How would we proceed to make such an inquiry? Where would we go to check facts? What is a "fact," anyway? How would we proceed in uncovering prejudice? On what basis would we judge a conclusion unjustifiable?

Professor Hirsch worries about such an approach, indeed, condemns it, because he believes that by learning about learning, students are deflected from getting the facts that "educated" people must have. But to proceed in this way permits students to learn "facts" and "truths" in the text as one hopes they will, and it also permits them to learn how to defend themselves against "facts" and "truths." Do we want our students to know what a noun is? The text will tell them, but that is the beginning of learning, not the end. Is the definition clear? Does it cover all cases? Who made it up? Has anyone come up with a different definition?

Do we want students to know what a molecule is? The text will tell them. But then the questions begin. Has anyone ever seen a molecule? Did the ancients believe in them? Was a molecule discovered or invented? Who did it? Suppose someone disbelieved in molecules, what then?

Do we want students to know about the causes of the Revolutionary War? A text will give some. But from whose point of view? And what sort of evidence is provided? What does objectivity mean in history? Is there no way to find out the "real" truth?

If students were occupied with such inquiries, they would inevitably discover the extent to which facts and truth have changed, depending upon the circumstances in which the facts were described and the truths formulated. They will discover how often humans were wrong, how dogmatically they defended their errors, how difficult it was and is to make corrections. Do we believe that our blood circulates through the body? In studying the history of biology, students will discover that 150 years after Harvey proved blood does circulate, some of the best physicians still didn't believe it. What will students make of the fact that Galileo, under threat of torture, was forced to deny that the Earth moves? What will students think if they acquaint themselves with the arguments *for* slavery in the United States?

Will our students become cynical? I think not—at least not if their education tells the following story: Because we are imperfect souls, our knowledge is imperfect. The history of learning is an adventure in overcoming our errors. There is no sin in being wrong. The sin is in our unwillingness to examine our own beliefs, and in believing that our authorities cannot be wrong.

Far from creating cynics, such a story is likely to foster a healthy and creative skepticism, which is something quite different from cynicism. It refutes the story of the student learner as the dummy in a ventriloquism act. It holds out the hope for students to discover a sense of excitement and purpose in being part of the Great Conversation.

Since I began this chapter with three ideas that were not taken as seriously as they were intended, I will end it with another one that is likely to have the same fate. I suggest the following test be given in each subject in the curriculum. We might think of it as the "final" exam:

Describe five of the most significant errors scholars have made in (biology, physics, history, etc.). Indicate why they are errors, who made them, and what persons are mainly responsible for correcting them. You may receive extra credit if you can describe an error that was made by the error corrector. You will receive extra extra credit if you can suggest a possible error in our current thinking about (biology, physics, history, etc.). And you will receive extra extra extra credit if you can indicate a possible error in some strongly held belief that currently resides in your mind.

Can you imagine this question being given on the SATs?

7 · The American Experiment

I have before me the Report of the New York State Curriculum and Assessment Council (dated April 1994). Its name will tell you, straight off, that reading it is likely to be a painful experience, since reports produced by councils are not known for easy comprehensibility, let alone literary style. Nonetheless, I have read it, and find in it the standard-brand stuff, meaning that it is filled with clichés, and thoroughly exhausted ones at that. The report is intended to bring to life (so it says) the recommendations "pursuant to *A New Compact for Learning* which was adopted by the Board of Regents in 1991." Among the "key principles" of this New Compact is the doctrine that "all children can learn," which leads one to suppose that the Old Compact assumed that only some children can learn, or maybe even only a few. Another of its key principles is that education should "aim at mastery," an idea that probably has never occurred to teachers before, and explains why thirty distinguished educators were needed to contribute their collective originality to the council. A third principle (there are only six) is that education should reward success and remedy failure, which is actually a fairly interesting principle if one is allowed to discuss it. For example, an argument can be made (didn't I come close to making it in the last chapter?) that we would do much better if we rewarded failure and remedied success.

I could go on in this petulant way, but it is not my intention to analyze this report. There can't be many people in the world, in the United States, maybe even New York State, who could care very much about what ideas the New York Board of Regents experts have come up with. But there is one idea that they *didn't* come up with that is worth the notice of many people. As an appendix to the report, there is included a list of forty-one goals directed toward "what children should be, know, and be able to do." The goals are stated in a form that specifies what students in elementary, middle, and secondary school must understand, acquire, develop, apply, respect, and practice. As you can imagine, there is plenty to be done here, including a few things that probably aren't any of the school's business. But putting that last phrase aside, students are expected, for example, to develop self-esteem, understand people of different cultural heritages, and develop knowledge and appreciation of the arts. There are many other goals along these lines with which no one could disagree. But there is one that is, as we say, conspicuous by its absence, at least to me. I refer to the goal of "acquiring and/or deepening a love of one's country." One would have thought that among forty-one goals designed for students going to school in America, and going to school free of charge, and pretty close to as long as they wish, at least one of them would concern promoting an affection, even if a muted one, for their country. There is, I must acknowledge, a goal that says students should acquire knowledge of the "political, economic, and social processes and policies in the United States at the national, state, and local levels." This strikes me as rather cold and distant language, especially when it is followed by a suggestion that students learn the same sort of thing about other countries.

There is, also, something about students' learning to respect civic values and acquiring attitudes necessary to participate in democratic self-government. I assume the authors of this goal would accept America as an example of democratic self-government, although they do not explicitly say so. And as for the attitudes necessary to participate in democratic self-government, they do not include respect, let alone affection, for America's traditions and contributions to world civilization. They do include a list of "values" students should accept, such as justice, honesty, self-discipline, due process, equality, and majority rule with respect for minority rights, each of which is not so much a "value" as it is a focal point of a great and continuous American argument about the meanings of such abstract terms. That students may not have an opportunity to learn about these arguments is suggested by the fact that nowhere included in the list of goals is that of acquiring knowledge of the history of America.

I have begun this way not because the education experts in New York State are unusual, but because they are typical. In their reluctance to include patriotism as a "value," they reflect a tendency throughout the country, a certain uneasiness about where patriotism might lead. There is certainly more emphasis, these days, on loving one's self than on loving one's country, which means, I suppose, that Philip Rieff was prophetic when he wrote about "the triumph of the therapeutic." In any case, this uneasiness about patriotism is at least understandable, since the idea of love of country is too easily transmogrified into a mindless, xenophobic nationalism, as in the instance of the patriots in Florida who insist on students' learning that America is superior to all other countries. I suspect that still another reason for steering clear of patriotism is the recent prominence of "revisionist" history, which has led to increased awareness of the uglier aspects of American history and culture. Teachers are likely to think that self-love or, indeed, love for cultures other than America is a safer and more wholesome route to take. But in steering clear of patriotism, educators miss an opportunity to provide schooling with a profound and transcendent narrative that can educate and inspire students of all ages. I refer, of course, to the story of America as a great experiment and as a center of continuous argument.

There are many ways to unveil this story, and good teachers, at every level, can think of several if they believe the story is worthwhile. The ideas below should be regarded as possibilities, but I would expect that whatever approach might be taken, every teacher would have read the following documents and books: Thomas Paine's *The Rights of Man,* the Declaration of Independence, the Constitution, Alexis de Tocqueville's *Democracy in America,* the Gettysburg Address, the Emancipation Proclamation, *The Adventures of Huckleberry Finn, The Scarlet Letter,* John Dewey's *Democracy and Education,* John F. Kennedy's inaugural address, and Martin Luther King, Jr.'s "I Have a Dream" speech.

If a teacher has not read this material, I would be reluctant to have him or her in close contact with American children. But assuming a teacher knows what these works signify, he or she might proceed by introducing some of the great experiments that characterize American culture, and which the rest of the world has looked upon with wonder. I should say there are four that will cover most of the important arguments Americans have had.

Like all experiments, each begins with a question. The first is, of course, Is it possible to have a coherent, stable culture that allows the greatest possible freedom of religious and political thought and expression? The origins of this question predate the founding of the United States, and how far back one should go in considering the question would depend on the age and experience of the students. I should think that fifth-grade students ought, at least, to learn about John Peter Zenger and the argument his Philadelphia lawyer, Andrew Hamilton, made on this question. (It might even help to pique student interest if they knew that the man who wanted Zenger put in jail for what he printed was named William —i.e., "Bill"—Cosby.) I should think fifth-, sixth-, and certainly seventh-grade students are capable of understanding some of the arguments made in the eighteenth century over the meanings of such words and terms as *freedom, equality, due process*, and *the divine right of kings*. As students advance in years, they may be introduced to less well known but significant arguments about the meanings of key concepts. De Tocqueville's distinction between egotism and individuality, both of which he thought dangerous, is a somewhat complex argument, but one worth having tenth or eleventh graders consider.

If it is "mastery" we are shooting for, I would hope no student would be allowed out of the eighth grade unless he or she knew by heart the First Amendment, which is, after all, the binding legal answer to the question concerning the permissible extent of freedom of expression (or perhaps not so much an answer as an hypothesis that is still being tested). I am aware that modern educators disapprove of students' being asked to memorize anything, classifying such a task under the dreaded rubric of "rote" learning. I stand with those who are against students' playing the "guess what answer I have in my head" game with teachers, but I do not think that such a stand rules out asking students to know by heart certain fundamental expressions of American ideals. There are, in any case, only forty-five words in the First Amendment, and I can't imagine that the brains of our students would be damaged by learning them, and in the order in which they are written. (The Gettysburg Address has fewer than 300 words, and I am told by teachers that memorizing them is quite beyond the capacity of many students, although if it were put to music, maybe they could manage it.)

I am neither qualified to give, nor desirous of giving, a history lesson, and still less a curriculum. I wish only to make three further points: First, and obviously, as students progress from elementary school to high school to college, the study of the American experiment in freedom of expression must deepen, the arguments considered must increase in complexity, and the documents containing them must be more various. Second, it should at all times be made clear that the arguments are not finished; that today they are pursued with the same passion they once were, especially those arguments that present a distinctly modern problem. Is pornography protected by the First Amendment? Does "freedom of the press" include television? Is prayer in the public schools a violation of the "establishment of religion" clause? These are arguable questions that, I should think, our students must know something about if they are to participate in the Great American Conversation. In fact, if an examination is required for students to show "mastery," then I suggest the following (let us say, to qualify for graduation from high school): Taking one of the current arguments about the meaning of the First Amendment, write an opinion on it as Thomas Paine (or Thomas Jefferson, or James Madison) might have argued the question. You must, of course, make reference to words they wrote and you may bring to class whatever documents you think you will require.

If this examination is judged too difficult, here is an alternative: Rewrite the First Amendment to include protections you think are necessary in today's world. Eliminate those you think are no longer necessary. You may wish neither to add nor subtract provisions, but to clarify words and phrases that are, at present, part of the First Amendment. Explain the reasons for the changes you make; or, if you make none, explain why none are needed.

If this one is too difficult, we might consider requiring the students to go back a few squares—that is, to do the twelfth grade one more time. It would be too dangerous to let them loose in a country that claims to be in favor of democratic self-government.

The third point that needs to be made is, of course, that there are nine more amendments comprising the Bill of Rights, most of which—especially the second, fourth, fifth, and sixth—have been the focus of intense argument from the beginning right up to the present. There are those, for example, who read the Second Amendment to mean that the government cannot prohibit citizens from owning weapons. There are others who think it means nothing of the sort. In July 1994, in a case receiving worldwide publicity (the O. J. Simpson double-murder trial), a judge was required to rule on a Fourth Amendment issue—whether or not certain evidence was illegally seized by detectives. There are law-enforcement officials who believe, a Supreme Court ruling to the contrary, that the Fifth Amendment is not violated if upon making an arrest they do not read Miranda rights to the suspect. The arguments go on, and everyone is entitled to participate. Is it too much to say that the arguments are the energy and the glory of the American experiment? Is it too much to hope that our young might learn to honor the tradition and to be inspired by it?

The second great American experiment began about the middle of the nineteenth century, and raised the following question: Is it possible to have a coherent, stable culture made up of people of different languages, religions, traditions, and races? Henry Adams thought the answer was no. Henry James agreed with him, and T. S. Eliot was so frightened at the thought he moved to England and stayed there. On the other hand, H. L. Mencken, of German heritage, believed that those who claimed to be white Anglo-Saxon Protestants not only weren't authentic WASPs but were thoroughly incompetent and no match intellectually for the "ethnics" who came in such numbers to America. But they did not come in equal numbers, in part because immigration laws assigned different values to different groups. And so from the beginning, there were arguments, and they continue to this day. Should America let everyone in? Are some groups better than others? If distinctions are made, on what basis should we make them? (Some of the early IQ tests showed Jews to be mentally deficient, giving support to an argument that restrictions be placed on the numbers of them allowed in.) Should English be the official language of America? And, of course, always, that most troublesome of all questions: What do we do to remedy the persistent effects of the legacy of slavery and discrimination from which an important segment of our population still suffers? Are they to be compensated for what was inflicted on them?

I do not say that the arguments over these questions are (or were) always rational. Behind many of them, there lurks fear or ignorance or (worse) misinformation. But as long as there is argument, there is the possibility of reducing fear, overcoming ignorance, correcting misinformation. Can anyone doubt that our students should know about the history of these arguments? What was it that made Henry Adams so unhappy? (If our students cannot read *The Education of Henry Adams*, a good teacher can summarize his argument.) What terrified T. S. Eliot? If students are going to be asked to read him, I would suggest that *Christianity and Culture* take precedence over his poetry. And if it is poetry we want, would it be too demanding to have Emma Lazarus's poem "The New Colossus" committed to memory? (The poem has been made into a song, which might make it as easy to learn as Bruce Springsteen's "Born in the USA.") The poem is, after all, an argument of sorts about what America should be. In any case, I have no doubt that teachers can find suitable material that conveys the idea that America as melting pot was, and still is, a vast social experiment about which there have been, and still are, disputes over its advantages and disadvantages. I should be astonished if American students do not have opinions on this matter which may be used to take them back into the past and forward into the future.

The third great experiment began toward the end of the nineteenth century, made all the more challenging by the reality of the second experiment, which resulted in a multicultural population. I refer to the question, Is it possible to provide a free public education for all citizens? Americans have not always agreed upon the desirability of doing this, although it has been nearly a century since anyone has made a respectable argument against it. Recently, there have emerged arguments in favor of privately run public schools (that is, free, or almost free, for students; profit-making for entrepreneurs). Its most vigorous exponent is Christopher Whittle, whose Edison Project, at this writing, claims to have contracts to manage three schools in Massachusetts, and hopes to have many more. He argues that a free-market approach to schooling will provide better education for the young. He is passionately opposed by the National Education Association, whose current president, Keith Geiger, says that Americans want "community-based, not corporate-imposed, education for their children."[1]

It is an interesting argument, and one whose outcome will have significant social and political implications. But the argument is not nearly as interesting, I think, as that which centers on what is meant, in the first place, by "education." I believe I am right in saying that teachers have been reluctant to introduce this question to students, although it is well within the intellectual range of high school students to consider. In fact, education as a subject of study is rarely taken seriously even in college, for reasons I find too painful to discuss. It is sufficient to say that many of the world's most esteemed philosophers have written extensively on education. Confucius and Plato were what we would call today "curriculum specialists." Cicero, Quintilian, Erasmus, Locke, Rousseau, and Thomas Jefferson wrote on the subject, and the great English poet John Milton was so moved by the prospect of writing an essay on education that he called the reforming of education "one of the greatest and noblest designs to be thought on." In modern times, such formidable intellects as William James, Bertrand Russell, Alfred North Whitehead, and, of course, John Dewey concerned themselves with education. Both Ludwig Wittgenstein and Karl Popper were elementary school teachers, and would of necessity have thought deeply about the subject.

The point is that there is a mass of material about what education means and how it should be conducted. And Americans have produced a good deal of it, since it was they who invented the idea of mass education, and they have been especially passionate in arguing about how their young citizens ought to be treated in school. We have here, then, a rich and inspiring set of arguments with which our students should be acquainted. Experienced teachers will know how and when to do this, but the following ideas ought to be kept at the forefront: first, that since these arguments concern *them* (that is, the students)—what they are capable of understanding, what interests them, how they will change—they are entitled to be heard on the matter. Second, while it is possible to speak wisely about education, no one can speak definitively. Third, there is no intellectual activity more American than quarreling about what education means, especially within the context of school. Americans rely on their schools, even more than on their courts, to express their vision of who they are, which is why they are usually arguing over what happens in school.

As with two of the other great experiments, the fourth one began in the nineteenth century but has taken on furious force in the twentieth. It raises the following question: Is it possible to preserve the best of American traditions and social institutions while allowing uncontrolled technological development? Some readers will know that I have addressed this question in previous writings and have allied myself with, among others, Lewis Mumford and Jacques Ellul in answering no. But I am aware that there are many serious and brilliant social critics who say yes. More than that, most Americans seem to say yes, although, if I am not mistaken, there is a creeping uneasiness among them that they may have answered too hastily. In any case, there is an experiment going on in America and it is being monitored carefully by people around the world. Since most industrialized nations are beginning to confront the question in the context of their own institutions and traditions, they look to what is happening in America as a source of guidance. Sometimes they find the experiment chilling, sometimes glorious. That the question generated by the experiment should be introduced to American students is rather obvious. The answers to the question will have a powerful impact on their lives; yet many of our young are not even aware that there is a question here, that there is anything to argue about. One may, then, have to start from the beginning. Let us say, with science fiction. Mary Shelley, Aldous Huxley, George Orwell, and Ray Bradbury are relevant authors who sound warnings about the dangers of an obsession with technology. Edward Bellamy (*Looking Backward*), B. F. Skinner (*Walden II*), and Arthur Clarke (*2001*) present a more hopeful outlook. I trust I have not loaded the case against technological optimism. If I have, add to the list of hopefuls almost any of Alvin Toffler's books, including his classic, *Future Shock*, which is not intended as science fiction, although it reads as if it is.

Of course, in one sense, we have here an old argument; people have always worried about whether technology demeans or enriches our humanity. In the nineteenth century, William Blake, for example, wrote about the "dark Satanic mills" that stripped men of their souls. Matthew Arnold warned that "faith in machinery" was humanity's greatest menace. Carlyle, Ruskin, and William Morris railed against the spiritual degradation brought by industrial progress. On the other hand, Mark Twain thought industrial progress was wonderful, and he once congratulated Walt Whitman on having lived in the age that gave the world the beneficial products of coal tar. More recently, C. P. Snow made what he regarded as a definitive answer to technological pessimists. He remarked that the industrial revolution, made possible by advanced technology, was the only hope for the poor. Their lives were rescued from centuries-old degradation by technology. Can anyone deny it?

In our own time, the argument has shifted from the effects of machinery to the effects of electronic impulses. Because the argument is relatively new, some of the questions are not yet well formulated. And in one notable case, a question was asked that was falsely assumed by many to be an answer. I refer to the question Marshall McLuhan posed: How does the structure of a medium alter the ways in which people "sense" the world? McLuhan himself offered many speculative answers, some of them wild and crazy, and thus led many to quarrel over his answers rather than to consider his question. But anyone who has carefully read his *Understanding Media* will know that this is a book of queries, intended to generate an interest in the *forms* of human communication; will also know that McLuhan believed, as I do, that our young are well suited to address such queries. They are not (to use one of McLuhan's puns, borrowed, I believe, from James Joyce) as "ABCED-minded" as their teachers are apt to be, and therefore they can see the effects, especially of nonprint media, more clearly than bookish folks. I am assuming here that teachers are bookish. If I am wrong about this, I prefer not to think about its implications.

In any case, questions raised about the effects of media and the diverse forms in which information is now packaged have relevance to all the other arguments now under way in America. Do television and computer technology limit or expand opportunities for authentic and substantive freedom of expression? Do new media create a global village, or force people to revert to tribal identities? Do new media make schools obsolete, and create new conceptions of education?

I acknowledge that questions like these have generally been barred from high school classrooms and students have had to wait until college or even graduate school before confronting them. This is a mistake, for two reasons. First, because, as I have said, teenage youth are knowledgeable about the varieties of media available in American culture and are likely to have refreshing insights into their effects. Second, as I have also said, they are apt to be unaware of the fact that there are serious arguments being made about the advantages and disadvantages of their media-made world, and they are entitled to be informed about and heard on the matter.

And there is one other point to be made: The approach I have outlined here—the study of the arguments about freedom of expression, about a melting-pot culture, about the meaning of education for an entire population, and about the effects of technology—is not simply a theme around which to organize a school curriculum. I mean to say that this is a powerful story that is at the core of what America is about. The story says that experimenting and arguing is what Americans do. It does not matter if you are unhappy about the way things are. Everybody is unhappy about the way things are. We experiment to make things better, and we argue about what experiments are worthwhile and whether or not those we try are any good. And when we experiment, we make mistakes, and reveal our ignorance, and our timidity, and our naïveté. But we go on because we have faith in the future— that we can make better experiments and better arguments. This, it seems to me, is a fine and noble story, and I should not be surprised if students are touched by it and find in it a reason for learning.

8 · The Law of Diversity

In his vast study of democracy in America, Alexis de Tocqueville concluded that all our political problems end up in the courts. Had there existed a public school system when he wrote, he might have added that all America's social problems end up in school. Are students insufficiently motivated to learn? Are they confused about or ignorant of the moral aspects of sex? Do they drive cars badly? Do they need psychological counseling? Are they uninformed about the dangers of drugs, alcohol, smoking, AIDS?

In America, it becomes the school's business to do something about these things. Of course, we have ample evidence that the schools do not do them very well, and there are those who believe that by assigning the schools the task of solving intractable social problems, we turn them into well-funded garbage dumps. This is a rather gross way to state the objection, frequently made by people of ill will. But there is, nonetheless, a reasoned complaint against the schools' trying to do what other social institutions are supposed to do but don't. The principal argument is that teachers are not competent to serve as priests, psychologists, therapists, political reformers, social workers, sex advisers, or parents. That some teachers might wish to do so is understandable, since in this way they may elevate their prestige. That some would feel it necessary to do so is also understandable, since many social institutions, including the family and church, have deteriorated in their influence. But unprepared teachers are not an improvement on ineffective social institutions; the plain fact is that there is nothing in the background or education of teachers that qualifies them to do what other institutions are supposed to do. It should be clear, by the way, that in this argument the phrase "unprepared teachers" does not mean that teachers cannot do *their* work. It means they cannot do *everyone's* work.

Having noted this, I hasten to say that it is not likely that Americans will change their views of school responsibilities, especially at a time when the potency of other institutions is problematic. Among the more controversial efforts along these lines is the attempt by some schools to ensure that students cultivate a deep sense of ethnic pride, a task once undertaken mostly by the family. I have, earlier, revealed that I think this to be a bad idea—to the extent that it subordinates or ignores the essential task of public schools, which is to find and promote large, inclusive narratives for all students to believe in. The principle of diversity is such a narrative and it is sometimes, strangely, confused with the idea of ethnic pride. To promote the understanding of diversity is, in fact, the opposite of promoting ethnic pride. Whereas ethnic pride wants one to turn inward, toward the talents and accomplishments of one's own group, diversity wants one to turn outward, toward the talents and accomplishments of all groups. Diversity is the story that tells of how our interactions with many kinds of people make us into what we are. It is a story strongly supported by the facts of human cultures. It does not usurp the function or authority of other social institutions. It does not undermine ethnic pride, but places one's ethnicity in the context of our common culture. It helps to explain the past, give clarity to the present, and provide guidance for the future. It is, in short, a powerful and inspiring narrative available for use in our public schools.

Among the many expressions of cultural diversity, there are four that stand out as of particular importance: language, religion, custom, and art and artifacts. Each of these may be thought of as a major subject or theme capable of revealing how difference contributes to increased vitality and excellence, and, ultimately, to a sense of unity.

Language

To give prominence to the study of the history of the English language cannot fail to offer students a clear view of the significance of diversity, and it is a wonder to me that those who speak passionately about the importance of diversity have not thought of this. As I have previously noted, English is the most multicultural language on Earth, and anyone who speaks it is indebted to people all over the world. It has been said, for example, that English is merely the French language pronounced badly. A wild exaggeration, of course, probably uttered by an embittered Frenchman. But, in fact, the English language has taken thousands of words from the French, beginning in the twelfth century. To take one small example: Almost all the words we use in law come from French—*bail, bailiff, jury, larceny, embezzle, perjury.* On the other hand, it might also be said that English is merely the German language pronounced badly, starting, as it did, as a Teutonic tongue. Or we may say that English comes from the Danish language. Almost all modern English words with an *sk* sound, such as *skill, skim, scare,* and *sky* are of Scandinavian origin, and it is more than likely that our words *man, wife, house, life, winter,* and many verbs—*to see, to hear, to ride, to sit,* and *to stand*—are also of Scandinavian origin.

How these words came to be part of English is a result of multiple invasions and conquests. Diversity sometimes comes at a heavy price. The Angles, Saxons, and Jutes (from northern Germany) invaded Britain, which was a province of the Roman Empire, drove out the Celts, and spoke the language we call Anglo-Saxon. In the eighth century, the Danes came, saw, and conquered. In the eleventh century, the Normans arrived. Otto Jespersen, one of the preeminent scholars of the history of English, and himself a Dane, wondered why most English words for meat *before* it is cooked are of Saxon origin—for example, *cow, swine, sheep,* and *calf*—while most of our words for meat *after* it is cooked are of Norman origin—*beef, pork, mutton,* and *veal.* His explanation: Since the Normans conquered the Saxons, the Saxons became their servants. In the kitchen, they used their own words; in the dining room, they were required to use Norman words. (This still leaves one mystery: Our word *breakfast* is of Saxon origin; *dinner* and *supper* are of Norman origin. Perhaps the Normans didn't eat until noon?)

To study the history of the English language is, therefore, to study the history of English-speaking peoples, or vice versa, which is the way I think it might be done if we wish to stress the importance of cultural interactions. I cannot say at what age students ought to begin the study of the history of English in ways that stress its multicultural dimensions. I know it can be done in the seventh grade, since I have done it.

Keeping an old teacher's tendency toward nostalgia under tight control, I can remember, nonetheless, the enthusiasm and even wonder of seventh graders discovering, first, the origins of their own names and then the various sources of the names of common foods. The latter assignment asked the students to imagine that four of them went to a local diner for lunch and gave the following orders: The first wanted soup, a cheeseburger with squash, and coleslaw on the side, then some tea with cherry pie. The second wanted a waffle, a banana split (this was years ago, when everyone knew what a banana split was), and coffee. The third wanted chili with plenty of pepper, and a cookie. The fourth ordered a turkey sandwich with gravy and soy sauce, and a Coke. The task was to discover the languages from which each of these food names originated. *Soup* derives from French; *cheese* comes from Latin; *burger* from German; *squash*, American Indian; *cole slaw*, Dutch; *tea*, Chinese; *cherry*, German; *pie*, Irish; *waffle*, Dutch; *banana*, African; *coffee*, Arabic; *chili*, Spanish; *pepper*, Indian; *cookie*, Dutch; *turkey*, Arabic; *gravy*, French; *soy*, Japanese; *Coke*, American. (I didn't include *pizza* because I thought it was too obvious.)

The imagined lunches may not have been nutritious for the body, but were for the mind. The assignment led us into a reasonably sophisticated study of the growth of English and its debt to languages all over the globe. The study may be called "etymology," or "historical linguistics," or, simply, "origins." Perhaps "origins" in elementary school because it is less frightening; "etymology" in high school; "historical linguistics" in college. The name is not important; the inquiry is.

It is possible that the subject can be introduced even earlier than the seventh grade, since most children are interested in where words come from. It is also well to keep in mind Jerome Bruner's famous dictum (from his *The Process of Education*) that any subject can be taught in an intellectually respectable way to children of almost any age.

American English is especially well suited to a celebration of the virtue of diversity, since the multicultural influences on it have been continuous and powerful. There is no group that ever came to America, or was here before anyone came, that has not contributed words, and therefore ideas, to the language. I recall the astonishment of an African-American student upon her discovery that the word *hominy* is a North American Indian word. This fact sparked her interest in tracking words of African-American origin (here indeed was ethnic pride, but within the context of diversity). There are many such words and she may, to this day, still be trying to pin down the origin of *juke* (as in jukebox), which seems to have come from black musicians in New Orleans, but nobody is sure.

Walt Whitman wrote that "the new times, the new people, the new vistas need a new tongue," and added, "yes, and what is more, they will have such a new tongue." He was right. But we did it by borrowing from every language that made itself available, including hundreds of names of rivers, mountains, towns, and regions taken from American Indians. We also did it through the agency of slang. Slang is a form of colloquial speech that has a bad reputation, largely perpetuated by schoolteachers. They have a point, since slang is almost always created in a spirit of defiance, which is why its most consistent creators are those from disaffected groups, people with grievances. Perhaps the most creative sources of American-English slang in our own time are African-Americans, who are particularly adept at reversing traditional meanings—*bad* becomes *good*, as does *funky* and *fat*. A woman who is looking especially good may be said to be "fat plus biscuits and gravy," and something may be so "cool," it is "hot." Aggrieved women, oppressed homosexuals, confused immigrants, and, of course, radical students have richly endowed the language with new words and new meanings for old ones. The words *mob, chum, crony,* and *snob* come to us from university students early in this century. And new terms keep coming. Linguistic diversity, in other words, comes not only from other languages but from the variety of social and regional dialects within our own language. It does not take very long when studying the origins of English words before one realizes how much is owed to the principle of diversity.

But I do not think it is sufficient for our students to know only the English language. If we are serious about making diversity a central narrative in the schooling of the young, it is necessary for our students to learn to speak at least one language other than English fluently. This sort of thing has been said many times before, and for a long time, but, I fear, has not been accomplished, or indeed even tried. Our failure is something of a worldwide embarrassment. The standard joke in other countries: What do we call someone who speaks three languages? Trilingual. Two languages? Bilingual. One language? An American. There are several reasons why we have failed to accomplish the task of teaching other languages, including starting too late (in high school), bad foreign-language teaching, and the nearly complete sufficiency of English for thousands of miles in every direction. There is even a political movement to discourage the use of foreign languages among our citizens by making English the "official" language of America. This is another one of those ideas borrowed from the French, who are obsessed with protecting their language and who even have an official academy to help keep it pure. But the English language needs no help in this way. English is not only the unchallenged language of America but is rapidly becoming the second language of the rest of the world. Nonetheless, this idea of an "official" language has possibilities—if the intention is to ensure that everyone will learn to speak it. Suppose we made, let us say, French our "official" language for fifteen years, then Japanese for the next fifteen. The English language would still be spoken by nearly everyone, but in thirty years, we would all be trilingual. Put that idea aside (you have already done so), although it may take an almost equally desperate idea to get us to pursue in a serious way foreign-language learning.

The reasons for serious foreign-language learning are many and various. First among them is that a foreign language provides one with entry into a worldview different from one's own. Even a language as similar to English in structure and vocabulary as Spanish will give different connotations to ideas and things, and therefore will suggest that the world is not exactly as the English language depicts it. Of course, languages such as Japanese, Chinese, and Russian will reveal this fact much more precisely. If it is important that our young value diversity of point of view, there is no better way to achieve it than to have them learn a foreign language and, it should go without saying, to begin to learn it as early as possible—in the first grade, for example.

One might also add that in preparing our young for the twenty-first century, bilingualism (at least) would seem to be a necessity. For some reason which is unknown to me, educational visionaries do not stress this point. They insist that competence in using computers is essential in a global economy, apparently believing that speaking a foreign language is not; at least one does not hear the importance of foreign-language learning spoken of very much. As I have already said, almost everyone is in the process of learning to use computers, irrespective of how much attention is given to the task in school. But if our schools pay little attention to foreign-languages, about 80 percent of our population will remain monolingual (at present about 32 million Americans speak a foreign tongue, leaving more than 200 million who do not). I suppose that if one must be monolingual, English is quite satisfactory, since it embodies the worldviews of so many different languages. But the point is that our young ought not to be monolingual, and if the schools paid less attention to driver education and other such marginal tasks, our students wouldn't be.

Religion

I am aware (who isn't?) that the words *religion* and *public schools* do not go together. Not in America. They are like magnets that, upon getting too close, repel each other. There are good reasons for this, among them the First Amendment, which, even before it mentions freedom of speech, prohibits Congress from establishing a national religion. This has been wisely interpreted to mean that public institutions may not show any preference for one religion over another. It has also been taken to mean, not so wisely, that public institutions should show no interest in religion at all. One consequence of this latter meaning is that public schools are barely able to refer to religion in almost any context.

It was not always so. I vividly recall singing Christmas carols in assembly when I was in public elementary school. About 60 percent of the students were Jewish, but this did not prevent them from singing enthusiastically, and in tune. I do not remember anyone's protesting, although Harold Posner and I took pleasure in amending some of the words ("Deck the halls with rows of challah"). We were trying to be cute, not defiant. I believe we thought "Silent Night," "Hark! The Herald Angels Sing" (naturally, we sang, "Hark! All Harold's Angels Sing"), and "Joy to the World" were merely American songs without religious significance. And I even suspect that most of the Catholic students thought the same. I do not speak of Protestants, since in my neighborhood they were too few in number to draw conclusions about, although I do remember that Henrietta Gutmann, a Lutheran, always had a mysterious, faraway look in her eyes when we sang "Silent Night." This worried me a little, as it hinted that there might be something there that I was missing.

The situation appears to be different these days. Jews, Muslims, Hindus, Buddhists, and atheists do not want Christian rituals, including songs, to be imposed on them—that is, to be given preference over their own rituals. I feel quite sure Thomas Paine and Thomas Jefferson would agree with them on this point, and so do I. But it does not follow from this that the public schools should ignore religion altogether.

There are several reasons for this, all of them obvious. One is that so much of our painting, music, architecture, literature, *and* science are intertwined with religion. It is, therefore, quite impossible (impossible by definition) for anyone to claim to be educated who has no knowledge of the role played by religion in the formation of culture. Another reason is that the great religions are, after all, the stories of how different people of different times and places have tried to achieve a sense of transcendence. Although many religious narratives provide answers to the questions of how and when we came to be, they are all largely concerned to answer the question, Why? Is it possible to be an educated person without having considered questions of why we are here and what is expected of us? And is it possible to consider these questions by ignoring the answers provided by religion? I think not, since religion may be defined as our attempt to give a total, integrated response to questions about the meaning of existence.

A third reason, related to the second and especially relevant to understanding the principle of diversity, is that by studying religion, our students can become acquainted with, first, the variety of ways people have offered to explain themselves and, second, the astonishing unity of their explanations. I therefore propose that beginning sometime in late elementary school and proceeding with focused detail in high school and beyond, we provide our young with opportunities to study comparative religion. Such studies would promote no particular religion but would aim at illuminating the metaphors, literature, art, and ritual of religious expression itself.

Can such a thing be done? Only, I imagine, very delicately. We would certainly need to be more tactful than teachers are inclined to be toward "Greek mythology." If you will allow still one more reference to my own school days, I recall being aware, in the eighth grade, that something was not quite right about our teacher's attitude toward the gods of the ancient Greeks, who were able to do miraculous things, including racing across the sky in a chariot. I knew that Jews believed their God had parted the Red Sea, and Christians believed their Savior died and came back to life. I was puzzled about why our teacher called the story of Greek gods "myth" but, I felt sure, would not so designate our own stories. I asked a Greek classmate named Nicholas (I've forgotten his family name) about this. He shrugged, told me his family was Greek Orthodox, and led me to believe he didn't care one way or the other. But those in charge of the education of our youth cannot be as cavalier as Nicholas. Of course, in proceeding, we would do away with the words *myth* and *mythology*. Perhaps in college the words can be restored in the sense that Joseph Campbell and Rollo May use them. But they are too laden with connotations of something that is false or mere superstition to use with younger students. What we must aim for is to provide every group's narrative with dignity; with a sense that it is a creative means of expressing mysteries of life; that its "truths" are different from those of science and journalism;

indeed, that it addresses questions science and journalism are not equipped to answer.

To say that something must be done delicately does not mean it cannot be done. Of course it can, if we do it with mature preparation. We must proceed, for example, with the knowledge that many students and their parents believe *their* story is the literal truth. There is no need to dispute them. Nothing could be further from my mind than that comparative religion studies should aim at "narrative busting" or even, for that matter, a superficial cynicism. The idea is to show that different people have told different stories; that they have, at various times, borrowed elements from one another's narratives; that it is appropriate to treat the narratives of others with respect; and that, ultimately, all such narratives have a similar purpose. Is it insulting to reveal that the Jews borrowed from the Egyptians? The Christians from the Jews? The Muslims from the Christians and the Jews? Is there any cynicism in revealing that American Indian deities have a special relationship to the earth and sky, not found in Western religions but similar in many ways to ancient Greek deities? Is there anything threatening in learning about the religions of African tribes? Do we endanger anyone by showing that Gandhi's religious beliefs were influenced by those of Thoreau, and that Martin Luther King, Jr.'s ideas were influenced by Gandhi?

If the answer to these questions is a continuous yes, then I am disarmed and must drop the subject. But I think many will answer no, and agree that there is an obligation for us to take the world into account on such important matters, and that there are few better ways to inculcate a sense of tolerance and even affection for difference than to teach about the varieties of religious experience.

My proposal here should not be taken to mean that I fail to

appreciate the difficulties confronting teachers who wish students to learn something about the diversity of religion. For example, there will be students who believe not only that *their* narrative is "true," but that all others are false. How does one cope with that? I am not sure, but one might proceed, first, by making students aware of those religions that do not insist on an exclusive truth—for example, Bahai, which takes the view that the prophets of all religions spoke the truth, although in different words, with meanings suitable to the times in which they spoke. One may also avoid certain difficulties by taking an historical approach, which inevitably reveals the dynamic nature of religious belief. Even a cursory review of Roman Catholicism will show that its ideas have changed—for example, on celibacy, on abortion, on dietary rules, even on the Inquisition and on the treatment of poor Galileo. Neither is it difficult to show how Protestant sects have changed their views and how they differ from one another. Or that, because of irreconcilable differences about the proper manner of religious observance, Jews have divided themselves into many groups—Orthodox, Modern Orthodox, Very Orthodox, Almost Orthodox, Conservative, Very Conservative, Nearly Conservative, Reform, Not Quite Reform. (One is permitted, I believe, to make fun of one's own group.) The point is that there is nothing disrespectful, and everything honest, in showing students that even within religions that insist on an exclusive "truth," truths change. But, of course, this does not adequately address the fact that certain fundamental truths of each particular religion do not change. The Christians believe the Messiah came. The Jews believe the Messiah is yet to come. The Buddhists don't believe in a Messiah at all. The Hindus believe in reincarnation. The Muslims do not. What then? The answer to any student who believes that other religions are simply wrong (or, as the Christian apologist C. S.

Lewis put it, are more primitive) is that he or she may be right. But, as the First Amendment implies, we cannot be sure, and, therefore, while everyone is permitted to be sure in his or her own mind, no one is permitted to prevent anyone from disagreeing.

In this connection, it may be valuable for students to know, certainly upper high school students, that many of the Founding Fathers were deists—for example, Jefferson and Paine, both of whom believed deeply in an "Almighty God" but who were skeptical about (in Paine's case, vigorously opposed to) organized religion, especially the Christian, Jewish, and, as it was called in their day, Turkish (Muslim). Jefferson wrote a version of the Four Gospels in which he removed all of the "fanciful" and "superstitious" elements, retaining only the ethical components. It is said that when he was elected President, some Christians hid their Bibles, fearing that government policy would be directed against "God-fearing Christians." They knew little about Jefferson, and even less about the First Amendment. Thomas Paine was vilified for his *The Age of Reason*, in which he tried to show that many things in the Bible could not possibly be true, and that the differences among religious systems show that they must all be wrong. His views on the purposes of religious systems were, it seems to me, shallow, and yet *The Age of Reason* is one of the most religious books I have ever read.

The point here is that tolerance is irrelevant when there is universal agreement. When there is diversity of opinion, tolerance becomes, if you will, a god to serve. But there are several meanings to the word. I do not have in mind the sort of tolerance characterized by a silent superiority. That is surely better than a Pat Buchanan–like vocal and aggressive superiority. But in the education of our young, we are obliged to do much better. I mean to help promote a variety of tolerance that says, "If I had been raised as you have, if I had been in your situation, if I had been led to respect the symbols you do, then it is very likely I would believe as you do." This kind of tolerance does not require students to abandon their beliefs, or even to think they are wrong. It requires only that they understand that there are more things about heaven than are dreamt of in their religion.

Were we to make the subject of comparative religion part of the education of our youth, there would arise many questions and difficulties to which I have no answers, and, I feel sure, to which other teachers have no answers either. But our ignorance does not rule the subject out. I said earlier we must proceed with mature preparation. This implies that there need to be national, regional, and local teacher conferences and institutes devoted to the ways in which comparative religion might be taught, so that teachers can learn from one another what the difficulties might be and how to overcome them. Does this seem too much to ask? Why is it that nothing is easier to organize, is more well funded, and more well attended than a conference on how to teach computers, or even one on media literacy? Is it certain that teacher interest can be aroused only about technical or technological matters? Are we too stupid or fearful to discuss the opportunities offered by religious diversity? I don't think so.

Custom

To teach about the diversity of religion would seem laden with difficulties, especially because we have so little experience in doing it. By comparison, to teach about the diversity of national or ethnic customs seems easy and familiar. There is probably no elementary school in the United States, and few high schools, that have not had some celebration of diverse customs, often a day in which native dress, food, and music are displayed, eaten, and heard. No one can complain about this—at least not much. Such efforts do suggest to our students certain kinds of differences among peoples of the world; and, always, there is the vague implication that such differences are worthy of respect.

But there is also the smell of quaintness about these events, even a sense of superiority, as if while acknowledging difference, we should keep in mind that these clothes, this food, and this music are not quite real, merely examples of exotica.

I hope I am wrong about this. But I do not think I am wrong about the superficiality of such approaches. They rarely, if ever, penetrate to the more robust expressions of cultural difference. It is one thing to reveal that not all teenagers around the world think it adorable to wear baseball caps backward; it is another thing to reveal differences in beliefs about kinship, about the legitimate sources of authority, about gender roles, about the meaning of politics, of history, of the future.

To get seriously into the subject of the diversity of custom is, therefore, to forgo the pleasures of superficial charm and to study aspects of culture that, in truth, are likely to make students uncomfortable. Yet, I would urge it on the grounds of necessity. Do educators command our attention by their warnings that the twenty-first century is hard on our heels, that our technology has created not only a global economy but a global village? Then it is essential, I would think, that our youth learn something of the ways of others who occupy the village.

Earlier, I have discussed introducing, as a major subject, anthropology, of which the study of customs is a part. But it is also a part of sociology. I once had a conversation with Margaret Mead about the difference between the two subjects. She said that sociology grew out of anthropology, mostly because there were anthropologists who wanted to avoid the personal discomfort of studying "primitive" peoples in their faraway native habitats. They preferred to study the customs of people in, say, Omaha, Nebraska, rather than in the Trobriand Islands. The result was a new subject: sociology. I don't know if there is any truth in this. (Since I knew Margaret Mead as a sober scholar, I ruled out the possibility that she was pulling my leg.) But there is little doubt that the two subjects make similar inquiries: How do the people of a particular culture communicate with one another? How do they define law, truth, intelligence? How do they educate their young? What roles do they assign to the sexes? How do they organize kinship? What authority do they respect? What role does their history play?

I mention the connection between anthropology and sociology because the study of diverse customs need not confine itself to people of faraway places. In most American classrooms, the student population will embody several different traditions, and it is likely that there is widespread ignorance about some of them. A teacher who has, let us say, Latinos, Koreans, African-Americans, Greeks, and Italians in class has enough material to last several semesters. He or she has available what the anthropologists call "native informants," who can speak with some degree of authority about the beliefs and attitudes of their respective cultures. Of course, like all native informants, they will often try to conceal certain aspects of their culture and cannot be expected to be entirely objective.

It is the role of the teacher to provide objectivity, which means to guide the inquiry with as much open-mindedness as possible. This is especially important to do, and quite difficult, when the study concerns people who have not been "Americanized" or who have nothing to do with America—for example, if the inquiry has shifted away from the student population to the people of Singapore or Iraq or China. Until 1994, most Americans knew very little about Singapore. And then, an American teenager, convicted in Singapore of what most Americans would regard as a minor crime, was cruelly punished by caning. This event provides (that is, would have provided) a valuable opportunity to study cultural differences. How do the people of Singapore view crime, teenagers, democracy? How are their views different from those of Americans? Is it possible for a teacher, not to mention students, to be objective about such differences?

I think it is, in the following sense: Through an act of scholarly imagination, one tries to understand the meanings Singaporeans give to the relevant concepts, to grasp how such meanings hold the culture together, to find in these meanings, if not virtue, a sense of necessity. It helps greatly if one compares Singaporean meanings to American meanings of the same concepts. One usually finds a measure of arbitrariness in customary ways of thinking. This does not mean that there is no basis for judging one set of meanings to be better than another. It means that a culture's history, geography, economy, and religion shape what comes to be thought seemly, natural, even inevitable. Before rushing to judgment, one must make an honest attempt to *understand*, and to teach the young how to understand.

It is easier said than done. Imagine how difficult it would be for an American teacher to stay open-minded about Iraqi customs regarding women, or about the Chinese practice (by no means just recent) of aborting or killing female infants in the belief that females are less valuable than males. Primitive, barbaric, evil? But then what of the American custom of killing those convicted of certain crimes, not out of economic necessity, but for revenge? Primitive, barbaric, evil, a Chinese sociologist might say. Not the same thing, we might reply. If we could explain to you our situation, if you knew how we think about these things, if you could simply understand the phrase "an eye for an eye, a tooth for a tooth," you would see that this makes quite good sense. It is, in fact, an affirmation of the value of life, and an indispensable collective catharsis. Well, maybe.

I am not arguing here for or against the custom known as capital punishment. I am talking about what it means to be open-minded and about the ways in which various cultures might explain their customs. There is always time to decide if a culture's customs are wasteful, ignorant, inhuman. Such decisions should await a study of why they exist. In the course of such studies, students may discover that there are striking similarities in how different cultures justify what at first seem to be unjustifiable customs.

But these are dark matters, and although they must be part of the study of customs, they are by no means all of it. We ought to be examining, for example, marriage ceremonies, education systems, manners, and parent-child relations. Students usually find the last two of special interest. I recall the bemusement—bordering on wonder—of some American tenth graders upon learning that in Thailand, children of *any* age will not disagree with their parents, and that it is almost as bad to disagree with their teachers. I tried to convince them that this was an altogether splendid idea. In their attempts to convince me that these customs were inappropriate in America, they learned much about America, Thailand, themselves, and the richness of diversity. So did I.

Art and Artifacts

I do not wish to give the impression that art is to be taught solely or even mostly to support the principle of diversity. But in studying the creative arts, one inevitably learns the value of diversity—let us say it is an inescapable side effect. Imagine a concert that features Luciano Pavarotti, Placido Domingo, and José Carreras. Zubin Mehta conducts; Yo-Yo Ma and Itzhak Perlman are soloists. Imagine that, after the intermission, Leontyne Price sings Wagner, while James Levine conducts, after which Van Cliburn plays Chopin and Tchaikovsky. Besides the fact that it would be nearly impossible to get tickets for such a concert, it would also be impossible for those who got in not to notice the contributions of people from all over the world. (Including the composers, I count musicians from nine different countries.)

But the audience has not come for a lesson in diversity or even, if you prefer, the universality of Western music. Neither do people go to museums and plays and read novels and poetry to learn about the cosmopolitan nature of artistic creation. They do these things to nourish their souls. Art, it has been said, is the language of the heart, and if we teach about music, painting, architecture, and literature in schools, we ought to be doing it to help our youth understand that language so that it may penetrate to their hearts. That is a very difficult thing to do, and I will make no attempt to disguise the fact that, save for literature, I have little experience (that is, none) in teaching the arts for this purpose. I will, therefore, confine my remarks to certain additional reasons for taking the arts and a culture's artifacts more seriously than we are accustomed to doing. All of these reasons have to do with diversity in one way or another.

We may give prominence to the arts because their subject matter offers the best evidence we have of the unity and continuity of human experience. Painting, for example, is more than three times as old as writing, and contains in its changing styles and themes a fifteen-thousand-year-old record of the ascent of humanity. And in showing this, it reveals how different peoples at different times have chosen to say what is in their hearts—their fears, their exaltations, their questions. I realize that in suggesting that we include the study of the history of art forms, I am coming close to subsuming art under the heading of archaeology, but I see no problem in this as long as we keep in mind the multiple purposes of art education. Indeed, I would suggest we might go even further. I recommend a subject that, so far as I know, has never been taught in American public schools. I am referring to the study of museums—not only art museums but museums of all kinds; that is to say, we would broaden our view of art to include artifacts of various forms and meanings. Why such a subject? Because a museum is an answer to a fundamental question: What does it mean to be a human being?

No museum I know of, not even the British Museum, gives a complete answer to this question, and none can be expected to. Every museum gives only a partial answer. Each one makes an assertion about the nature of humanity—sometimes supporting and enriching one another's claims but just as often contradicting one another.

There is a great museum in Munich that is filled with old automobiles, trains, and airplanes, all of which are meant to signify that human beings are preeminently toolmakers and are at their best when solving practical problems. The Guggenheim Museum in New York City rejects that claim; there is nothing displayed in the Guggenheim that is, or ever was, of any practical value. The museum seems to argue that what makes us human is our need to express our feelings in symbolic forms. We are human precisely because so many of our creations are impractical. To this, the Imperial War Museum in London says, "Nonsense. You are both wrong. We are at our most human when devising ways to kill one another." To which Yad Vashem in Jerusalem adds with inconsolable sadness, "That is true. But we are not merely killers like sharks and tigers; we are cruel, pointless, and systematic killers. Remember this above all."

Go to any museum in the world, even one that serves only as an archive, and ask, "What is this museum's definition of humanity?" You will be rewarded with some kind of an answer. In some cases, the answer will be timid and even confused; in others, bold and unmistakable. Of course, it is folly to say which museums convey the right answers. All of them are correct: We *are* toolmakers and symbol makers and war makers. We are sublime and ridiculous, beautiful and ugly, profound and trivial, spiritual and practical. So it is not possible to have too many museums, because the more we have, the more detailed and comprehensive will be the portrait of humanity.

But in saying that every museum gives us part of the picture, I am not saying that every museum is equally useful. To paraphrase George Orwell, all museums tell the truth, but some tell more important truths than others. And how important a truth is depends on the time and place of its telling. For at different times, cultures need to know, remember, contemplate, and revere different ideas in the interest of survival and sanity. A museum that was useful fifty years ago might be quite pointless today. But I would never wish that such a museum be closed, for someday, in changed circumstances, its usefulness may be restored (and in any case, the dialectic of museums requires that all the voices be counted). Nonetheless, for a specific time and place, the truths conveyed by a particular museum can be irrelevant and even harmful. Scores of museums—some of them new—celebrate ideas that are not needed.

To help clarify my point, imagine that the year is 1933, that you have been given unlimited funds to create a museum in Berlin, and that it has not occurred to you that you might be shot or otherwise punished for anything you will do. What kind of museum would you create? What ideas would you sanctify? What part of the human past, present, or imagined future would you wish to emphasize, and what part would you wish to ignore? In brief, what would you want your German visitors to the museum to contemplate?

In asking these questions, I mean to suggest that a museum is, in a fundamental sense, a political institution. For its answers to the question, "What does it mean to be a human being?" must be given within the context of a specific moment in history and must inevitably be addressed to living people who, as always, are struggling with the problems of moral, psychological, and social survival. I am not urging that museums be used as instruments of cheap and blatant propaganda; I am saying that a museum is an instrument of survival and sanity. A museum, after all, tells a story. And like the oral and written literature of any culture, its story may serve to awaken the better angels of our nature or to stimulate what is fiendish. A museum can serve to clarify our situation or obfuscate it, to tell us what we need to know or what is useless.

In his *The Quintessence of Ibsenism*, George Bernard Shaw

tells us precisely why museums are necessary. He addressed the question, Why do we need theater? But his answer applies just as well to museums. He said, "It is an elucidator of social consciousness, a historian of the future, an armory against darkness and despair, and a temple in the ascent of man."

Can you imagine "museums" as a specific subject in high school or college? Can you imagine a high school or college *without* such a subject? I am perhaps expecting too much. But in case I am not, may I propose a project that asks students to write a prospectus for a new museum in their community. They would be required to indicate what the museum would try to say, as well as what objects of art, custom, and technology would best say it. Such a project might be the final exam of a year-long course devoted to an analysis of whatever museums are accessible in the community. The course would probably require two or three teachers working together, for it would certainly be, to paraphrase a notorious Iraqi leader, the mother of all interdisciplinary courses. But I believe it is not beyond the range of high school faculties, certainly not of college faculties, and I can think of few better approaches for demonstrating the great story of human diversity.

The study of museums is likely to lead students in many different directions, perhaps as much away from artistic creations as toward them. Artifacts are not necessarily art, and it is important to keep in mind that the study of the former is no substitute for the study of the latter. I referred earlier to art as the language of the heart. But not all hearts are equally open to the variety of languages in which art speaks. There are, as we know, different levels of sensibility. In the case of music, for example, most American students are well tuned to respond with feeling, critical intelligence, and considerable attention to forms of popular music, but are not prepared to feel or even to experience the music of Haydn, Bach, or Mozart; that is to say, their hearts are closed, or partially closed, to the canon of Western music. I am not about to launch into a screed against rock, metal, rap, and other forms of teenage music. In fact, readers should know that Roger Waters, once the lead singer of Pink Floyd, was sufficiently inspired by a book of mine to produce a CD called *Amused to Death*. This fact so elevated my prestige among undergraduates that I am hardly in a position to repudiate him or his kind of music. Nor do I have the inclination for any other reason. Nonetheless, the level of sensibility required to appreciate the music of Roger Waters is both different and lower than what is required to appreciate, let us say, a Chopin étude. And we have a somewhat similar situation in respect to other art forms. There is, in short, something missing in the aesthetic experience of our young.

The problem may be stated in the following way: Because of the nature of the communications industry, our students have continuous access to the popular arts of their own time—its music, rhetoric, design, literature, architecture. As a consequence, their receptivity to popular forms is well developed and appropriate. But their capacity to respond with educated imaginations to traditional or classical forms of art is severely limited.

What is to be done? In the interests of cultivating resourcefulness and diversity in levels of sensibility, I would say there is no excuse for schools to sponsor rock concerts when students have not heard the music of Mozart, Beethoven, Bach, or Chopin, or for students to have graduated from high school without having read, for example, Shakespeare, Milton, Keats, Dickens, Whitman, Twain, Melville, or Poe, or for students not to have seen at least a photograph of paintings by Goya, El Greco, David. It is not to the point that many of these composers, writers, and painters were in their own times popular artists. What is to the point is that they spoke, when they did, in a language and from a point of view different from our own. It is also to the point that the popular arts tend to mute the voices of these artists and render their standards of excellence invisible.

I am—to reiterate—not speaking against popular art forms. I am speaking against our allowing them to monopolize the souls of our students. So far as art education is concerned, our schools ought to serve as a "counterenvironment," as if to say, "The equipment you now have to respond to the arts is incomplete. Your capacity for nourishing your feeling life will be expanded and, yes, elevated."

This brings me to three highly charged arguments about the arts (and about culture): first, whether or not there are higher and lower levels of sensibility; second, whether or not the canons of literature and other art forms have legitimacy; and third, whether or not schools can justify transmitting, indeed celebrating, Eurocentric culture, especially as it is dominated by dead white males.

I can be brief, since I think that for all the sound and fury, there is not much to argue about. I have, for example, already given my answer to the first question, and I would only add that if there are not higher and lower levels of sensibility in responses to art, language, and other forms of human communication, then there is no need for education. This applies to intelligence as well. Even if there are, as Howard Gardner has postulated, various kinds of intelligences, we must assume that there are higher and lower expressions of each one. The task of a school is to increase students' capacities. That means to have them move from lower to higher modalities of thought and feeling.

As to the legitimacy of canons, the word simply refers to

agreed-upon examples of excellence in various genres of creativity. Any canon can be added to, modified, or even discarded if it no longer serves, in part or whole, as a model of excellence. This means that any canon is a living, dynamic instrument, and it is certainly not limited to those artists who are dead, and long dead. The long dead dominate for the obvious reason that their works have given pleasure and instruction to diverse people over long periods of time. They have earned, so to speak, their place. To the extent that teachers believe in the importance of conveying a sense of continuity in artistic creation, they must give respectful attention to the long dead. But, of course, teachers must not be reluctant to include models of excellence produced by living artists. If teachers know of better examples of Western dramatic art than have been provided by Shakespeare, Molière, Ibsen, Shaw, Williams, and O'Neill, then they must let us know about it and explain why they think it so. If there are better examples of symphonic music than those produced by Beethoven, Brahms, Mozart, and Tchaikovsky, then we should hear them, along with explanations as to why they should be preferred.

A problem does arise, however, when someone injects a confusing, irrelevant point into the argument. I refer, for example, to Saul Bellow's rhetorical question concerning the absence of Swahili novels (or was it Navajo novels?) that are the equal or superior to the novels of Proust. I think he meant to justify Proust's place in the canon and to ridicule the largely political motive of including Third World writers on the list. Of course, if we are talking about the canon of the genre known as novels, then Bellow has a point. There are no Swahili or Navajo novelists who will threaten Proust's place in the canon (although there may be Chinese or Japanese novelists who do). But the speakers of Swahili or Navajo and scores of other languages do not normally write the kind of literature we call novels. They express themselves in other genres, often associated with the oral tradition. There is, I am sure, a canon (that is, examples of excellence) in every form of literature from Navajo poetry to Japanese Noh dramas. In the interest of diversity, our students ought to experience some of these forms, and teachers may introduce them as additions to the conceptions of excellence developed in our own culture.

I should add that the remarks above are not intended to suggest that art and especially literature teachers should confine themselves, and their students, to models of excellence. There are many reasons to ask students to read a particular book, and only one of them is that the book is an exemplary example of literary art. Teachers may choose even badly written books if such books are of sociological or political interest. At the same time, there are books that have earned a place in the canon but are not suitable for students at a particular stage in their development. (Proust in high school? Not a good idea.) The main point, however, is that teachers ought to have a *conception* of models of excellence; indeed, they are obliged to.

Last, there is the nonproblem of the dead white males. I believe it was Camille Paglia who remarked that if not for the dead white males, we would all be living in grass huts. A more refined but equally definitive comment was made by James Earl Jones (when interviewed by Charlie Rose). He noted that, for good or ill, our culture was formed from the religion, politics, literature, science, technology, philosophy, and art of mostly dead white males who lived in Europe and Asia Minor. There is, he said, no use pretending otherwise. What the dead white males gave us is now being enacted, criticized, and re-created by living black males, by living white females, and by several other interesting combinations, including quite a number of living white males. I should not be taken to mean that the cultures of dead Chinese or dead Africans ought to be ignored. Anyone who has urged that anthropology and archaeology be major subjects in school must be exempt from the charge of cultural chauvinism. I would add that in the interest of a robust diversity, studies of Asian, African, and other significant cultures would be highly desirable, provided they were available to all students. I am keeping in mind that the purpose of public education is to help the young transcend individual identity by finding inspiration in a story of humanity.

Meanwhile, it is well to remember that (by my count and my canons) the dead white males who gave us our religious, scientific, and artistic traditions came from at least thirty-seven different cultures. They were as diverse a group as one could imagine. Could there be any two people more different than Jesus and Martin Luther? Than Kepler and Einstein? Than Milton and Cervantes? Than Dostoyevsky and Emerson? Nonetheless, it was they who somehow taught us that diversity is a great and noble principle. If anyone has argued persuasively to the contrary, I haven't heard of it.

9 · The Word Weavers/
The World Makers

In an effort to clear up confusion (or ignorance) about the meaning of a word, does anyone ask, What is *a* definition of this word? Just about always, the way of putting the question is, What is *the* definition of this word? The difference between *a* and *the* in this context is vast, and I have no choice but to blame the schools for the mischief created by an inadequate understanding of what a definition is. From the earliest grades through graduate school, students are given definitions and, with few exceptions, are not told whose definitions they are, for what purposes they were invented, and what alternative definitions might serve equally as well. The result is that students come to believe that definitions are *not* invented; that they are not even human creations; that, in fact, they are—how shall I say it?—part of the natural world, like clouds, trees, and stars.

In a thousand examinations on scores of subjects, students are asked to give definitions of hundreds of things, words, concepts, procedures. It is to be doubted that there are more than a few classrooms in which there has been any discussion of what a definition is. How is that possible?

Let us take the equally strange case of questions. There will be no disagreement, I think, to my saying that all the answers given to students are the end products of questions.

Everything we know has its origin in questions. Questions, we might say, are the principal intellectual instruments available to human beings. Then how is it possible that no more than one in one hundred students has ever been exposed to an extended and systematic study of the art and science of question-asking? How come Alan Bloom didn't mention this, or E. D. Hirsch, Jr., or so many others who have written books on how to improve our schools? Did they simply fail to notice that *the principal intellectual instrument available to human beings is not examined in school?*

We are beginning to border on absurdity here. And we cross the line when we consider what happens in most schools on the subject of metaphor. Metaphor does, in fact, come up in school, usually introduced by an English teacher wanting to show how it is employed by poets. The result is that most students come to believe metaphor has a decorative function and only a decorative function. It gives color and texture to poetry, as jewelry does to clothing. The poet wants us to see, smell, hear, or feel something concretely, and so resorts to metaphor. I remember a discussion, when I was in college, of Robert Burns's lines: "O, my love is like a red, red rose / That's newly sprung in June. / O my love is like the melodie / That's sweetly play'd in tune."

The first questions on the test were: "Is Burns using metaphors or similes? Define each term. Why did Burns choose to use metaphors instead of similes, or similes instead of metaphors?"

I didn't object to these questions at the time except for the last one, to which I gave a defiant but honest answer: How the hell should I know? I have the same answer today. But today, I have some other things to say on the matter. Yes, poets use metaphors to help us see and feel. But so do biologists, physicists, historians, linguists, and everyone else who is trying to say something about the world. A metaphor is not an ornament. It is an organ of perception. Through metaphors, we see the world as one thing or another. Is light a wave or a particle? Are molecules like billiard balls or force fields? Is history unfolding according to some instructions of nature or a divine plan? Are our genes like information codes? Is a literary work like an architect's blueprint or a mystery to be solved?

Questions like these preoccupy scholars in every field. Do I exaggerate in saying that a student cannot understand what a subject is about without some understanding of the metaphors that are its foundation? I don't think so. In fact, it has always astonished me that those who write about the subject of education do not pay sufficient attention to the role of metaphor in giving form to the subject. In failing to do so, they deprive those studying the subject of the opportunity to confront its basic assumptions. Is the human mind, for example, like a dark cavern (needing illumination)? A muscle (needing exercise)? A vessel (needing filling)? A lump of clay (needing shaping)? A garden (needing cultivation)? Or, as so many say today, is it like a computer that processes data? And what of students? Are they patients to be cared for? Troops to be disciplined? Sons and daughters to be nurtured? Personnel to be trained? Resources to be developed?

There was a time when those who wrote on the subject of education, such as Plato, Comenius, Locke, and Rousseau, made their metaphors explicit and in doing so revealed how their metaphors controlled their thinking.[1] "Plants are improved by cultivation," Rousseau wrote in *Emile*, "and man by education." And his entire philosophy rests upon this comparison of plants and children. Even in such ancient texts as the Mishnah, we find that there are four kinds of students: the sponge, the funnel, the strainer, and the sieve. It will surprise you to know which one is preferred. The sponge, we are told, absorbs all; the funnel receives at one end and spills out at the other; the strainer lets the wine drain through it and retains the dregs; but the sieve—that is the best, for it lets out the flour dust and retains the fine flour. The difference in educational philosophy between Rousseau and the compilers of the Mishnah is precisely reflected in the difference between a wild plant and a sieve.

Definitions, questions, metaphors—these are three of the most potent elements with which human language constructs a worldview. And in urging, as I do, that the study of these elements be given the highest priority in school, I am suggesting that world making through language is a narrative of power, durability, and inspiration. It is the story of how we make the world known to ourselves, and how we make ourselves known to the world. It is different from other narratives because it is about nouns and verbs, about grammar and inferences, about metaphors and definitions, but it is a story of creation, nonetheless. Even further, it is a story that plays a role in all other narratives. For whatever we believe in, or don't believe in, is to a considerable extent a function of how our language addresses the world. Here is a small example:

Let us suppose you have just finished being examined by a doctor. In pronouncing his verdict, he says somewhat accusingly, "Well, you've done a very nice case of arthritis here." You would undoubtedly think this is a strange diagnosis, or more likely, a strange doctor. People do not "do" arthritis. They "have" it, or "get" it, and it is a little insulting for the doctor to imply that you have produced or manufactured an illness of this kind, especially since arthritis will release you from certain obligations and, at the same time, elicit sympathy from other people. It is also painful. So the idea that you have done arthritis to yourself suggests a kind of self-serving masochism.

Now, let us suppose a judge is about to pass sentence on a man convicted of robbing three banks. The judge advises him to go to a hospital for treatment, saying with an air of resignation, "You certainly have a bad case of criminality." On the face of it, this is another strange remark. People do not "have" criminality. They "do" crimes, and we are usually outraged, not saddened, by their doings. At least that is the way we are accustomed to thinking about the matter.

The point I am trying to make is that such simple verbs as *is* or *does* are, in fact, powerful metaphors that express some of our most fundamental conceptions of the way things are. We believe there are certain things people "have," certain things people "do," even certain things people "are." These beliefs do not necessarily reflect the structure of reality. They simply reflect an habitual way of talking about reality. In his book *Erewhon*, Samuel Butler depicted a society that lives according to the metaphors of my strange doctor and strange judge. There, illness is something people "do" and therefore have moral responsibility for; criminality is something you "have" and therefore is quite beyond your control. Every legal system and every moral code is based on a set of assumptions about what people are, have, or do. And, I might add, any significant changes in law or morality are preceded by a reordering of how such metaphors are employed.

I am not, incidentally, recommending the culture of the people of Erewhon. I am trying to highlight the fact that our language habits are at the core of how we imagine the world. And to the degree that we are unaware of how our ways of talking put such ideas in our heads, we are not in full control of our situation. It needs hardly to be said that one of the purposes of an education is to give us greater control of our situation.

School does not always help. In schools, for instance, we

find that tests are given to determine how smart someone *is* or, more precisely, how much smartness someone *has*. If, on an IQ test, one child scores a 138 and another a 106, the first is thought to *have* more smartness than the other. But this seems to me a strange conception—every bit as strange as "doing" arthritis or "having" criminality. I do not know anyone who *has* smartness. The people I know sometimes *do* smart things (as far as I can judge) and sometimes *do* dumb things—depending on what circumstances they are in, how much they know about a situation, and how interested they are. Smartness, so it seems to me, is a specific performance, done in a particular set of circumstances. It is not something you *are* or *have* in measurable quantities. In fact, the assumption that smartness is something you *have* has led to such nonsensical terms as *over-* and *underachievers*. As I understand it, an overachiever is someone who doesn't *have* much smartness but does a lot of smart things. An underachiever is someone who *has* a lot of smartness but does a lot of dumb things.

The ways in which language creates a worldview are not usually part of the schooling of our young. There are several reasons for this. Chief among them is that in the education of teachers, the subject is not usually brought up, and if it is, it is introduced in a cavalier and fragmentary fashion. Another reason is that it is generally believed that the subject is too complex for schoolchildren to understand, with the unfortunate result that language education is mostly confined to the study of rules governing grammar, punctuation, and usage. A third reason is that the study of language as "world-maker" is, inescapably, of an interdisciplinary nature, so that teachers are not clear about which subject ought to undertake it.

As to the first reason, I have no good idea why prospective teachers are denied knowledge of this matter. (Actually, I have *some* ideas, but a few of them are snotty and all are unkind.) But if it were up to me, the study of the subject would be at the center of teachers' professional education and would remain there until they were done—that is, until they retire. This would require that they become well acquainted with the writings of Aristotle and Plato (among the ancients), Locke and Kant (among recent "ancients"), and (among the moderns) I. A. Richards, Benjamin Lee Whorf, and, especially, Alfred Korzybski.

A few paragraphs about Korzybski are in order here, since his work offers the most systematic means of introducing the subject, deepening it, and staying with it. Another reason is that academics at the university level either do not know about Korzybski's work or, if they do, do not understand it (which does not mean, by the way, that fifth graders cannot). If they do understand it, they hate it. The result is that an exceedingly valuable means of exploring the relationship between language and reality goes unused.

Korzybski was born in Poland in 1879. He claimed to be of royal ancestry, referring to himself as Count Alfred Korzybski—another reason why academics have kept him at arm's length. He was trained in mathematics and engineering, and served as an artillery officer in World War I. The carnage and horror he witnessed left him haunted by a question of singular importance. He wondered why scientists could have such astonishing successes in discovering the mysteries of nature while, at the same time, the nonscientific community experienced appalling failure in its efforts to solve psychological, social, and political problems. Scientists signify their triumphs by almost daily announcements of new theories, new discoveries, new pathways to knowledge. The rest of us announce our failures by warring against ourselves and others. Korzybski began to publish his answer to this enigma in 1921 in his book *Manhood of Humanity: The Science and Art of Human*

Engineering. This was followed in 1926 by *Time-Binding: The General Theory,* and finally by his magnum opus, *Science and Sanity,* in 1933.

In formulating his answer, Korzybski was at all times concerned that his ideas should have practical applications. He conceived of himself as an educator who would offer to humanity both a theory and a method by which it might find some release from the poignant yet catastrophic ignorance whose consequences were to be witnessed in all the historic forms of human degradation. This, too, was held against him by many academics, who accused him of grandiosity and hubris. Perhaps if Korzybski had thought *smaller,* his name would now appear more frequently in university catalogues.

Korzybski began his quest to discover the roots of human achievement and failure by identifying a critical functional difference between humans and other forms of life. We are, to use his phrase, "time-binders," while plants are "chemistry-binders," and animals are "space-binders." Chemistry-binding is the capacity to transform sunlight into organic chemical energy; space binding, the capacity to move about and control a physical environment. Humans have these capacities, too, but are unique in their ability to transport their experience through time. As time-binders, we can accumulate knowledge from the past and communicate what we know to the future. Science-fiction writers need not strain invention in their search for interesting time-transporting machinery: *We* are the universe's time machines.

Our principal means of accomplishing the binding of time is the symbol. But our capacity to symbolize is dependent upon and integral to another process, which Korzybski called "abstracting." Abstracting is the continuous activity of selecting, omitting, and organizing the details of reality so that we experience the world as patterned and coherent. Korzybski shared with Heraclitus the assumption that the world is undergoing continuous change and that no two events are identical. We give stability to our world only through our capacity to re-create it by ignoring differences and attending to similarities. Although we know that we cannot step into the "same" river twice, abstracting allows us to act as if we can. We abstract at the neurological level, at the physiological level, at the perceptual level, at the verbal level; all of our systems of interaction with the world are engaged in selecting data from the world, organizing data, generalizing data. An abstraction, to put it simply, is a kind of summary of what the world is like, a generalization about its structure.

Korzybski might explain the process in the following way: Let us suppose we are confronted by the phenomenon we call a "cup." We must understand, first of all, that a cup is not a thing, but an event; modern physics tells us that a cup is made of billions of electrons in constant movement, undergoing continuous change. Although none of this activity is perceptible to us, it is important to acknowledge it, because by so doing, we may grasp the idea that *the world is not the way we see it.* What we see is a summary—an abstraction, if you will—of electronic activity. But even what we *can* see is not what we *do* see. No one has ever seen a cup in its entirety, all at once in space-time. We see only parts of wholes. But usually we see enough to allow us to reconstruct the whole and to act as if we know what we are dealing with. Sometimes, such a reconstruction betrays us, as when we lift a cup to sip our coffee and find that the coffee has settled in our lap rather than on our palate. But most of the time, our assumptions about a cup will work, and we carry those assumptions forward in a useful way by the act of naming. Thus we are assisted immeasurably in our evaluations of the world by our language, which provides us with names for the events that confront us and, by our naming them, tells us what to expect and how to prepare ourselves for action.

The naming of things, of course, is an abstraction of a very high order and of crucial importance. By naming an event and categorizing it as a "thing," we create a vivid and more or less permanent map of what the world is like. But it is a curious map indeed. The word *cup*, for example, *does not in fact denote anything that actually exists in the world*. It is a concept, a summary of millions of particular things that have a similar look and function. The word *tableware* is at a still higher level of abstraction, since it includes not only all the things we normally call cups but also millions of things that look nothing like cups but have a vaguely similar function.

The critical point about our mapping of the world through language is that the symbols we use, whether *patriotism* and *love* or *cups* and *spoons*, are always at a considerable remove from the reality of the world itself. Although these symbols become part of ourselves—Korzybski believed they become imbedded in our neurological and perceptual systems—we must never take them completely for granted. As Korzybski once remarked, "Whatever we say something *is*, it is not."

Thus, we may conclude that humans live in two worlds—the world of events and things, and the world of *words* about events and things. In considering the relationship between these two worlds, we must keep in mind that language does much more than construct concepts about the events and things in the world; it tells us what sorts of concepts we ought to construct. For we do not have a name for everything that occurs in the world. Languages differ not only in their names for things but in what things they choose to name. Each language, as Edward Sapir observed, constructs reality differently from all the others.

This, then, is what Korzybski meant by what he called general semantics: the study of the relationship between the world of words and the world of "not words," the study of the territory we call reality and how, through abstracting and symbolizing, we map the territory. In focusing on this process, Korzybski believed he had discovered why scientists are more effective than the rest of us in solving problems. Scientists tend to be more conscious of the abstracting process; more aware of the distortions in their verbal maps; more flexible in altering their symbolic maps to fit the world. His main educational objective was to foster the idea that by making our ordinary uses of language more like the scientific uses of language, we may avoid misunderstanding, superstition, prejudice, and just plain nonsense. Some of his followers, S. I. Hayakawa, Irving Lee, and Wendell Johnson, wrote readable texts for use in schools, but their material is not much in fashion these days. I wrote some texts along these lines myself, mostly to find out if these ideas are suitable for younger students, and discovered that they are. (I remember with delight the easy success we had with them in Arlington, Virginia, at the Fort Myer Elementary School.) But, of course, not all of the ideas are useful, and not all of them are good. General semantics, like any other system, has to be applied with a considerable degree of selectivity. Assuming teachers know something about the subject, they will discover what works and what doesn't. It is, in any case, a mistake to assume that profound ideas about language, from general semantics or any other place, cannot be introduced until graduate school.

Of course, there are plenty of "other places" from which profound ideas about language may come. The work of I. A. Richards (generally) and what he says, specifically, on definition and metaphor are good introductions to language as world-maker. On definition (from his *Interpretation in Teaching*):

I have said something at several places . . . about the peculiar paralysis which the mention of definitions and,
still more, the discussion of them induces. It can be prevented, I believe, by stressing the purposive aspect of
definitions. We want to do something and a definition
is a means of doing it. If we want certain results, then
we must use certain meanings (or definitions). But no
definition has any authority apart from a purpose, or to
bar us from other purposes. And yet they endlessly do
so. Who can doubt that we are often deprived of very
useful thoughts merely because the words which might
express them are being temporarily preempted by other
meanings? Or that a development is often frustrated
merely because we are sticking to a former definition of
no service to the new purpose?[2]

What Richards is talking about here is how to free our
minds from the tyranny of definitions, and I can think of no
better way of doing this than to provide students, as a matter
of course, with alternative definitions of the important concepts with which they must deal in a subject. Whether it be
molecule, fact, law, art, wealth, genes, or whatever, it is essential that students understand that definitions are instruments designed to achieve certain purposes, that the
fundamental question to ask of them is not, Is this the real
definition? or Is this the correct definition? but What purpose
does the definition serve? That is, Who made it up and why?

I have had some great fun, and so have students, considering the question of definition in a curious federal law. I refer
to what you may not say when being frisked or otherwise examined before boarding an airplane. You may not, of course,
give false or misleading information about yourself. But beyond that, you are also expressly forbidden to joke about any

of the procedures being used. This is the only case I know of where a joke is prohibited by law (although there are many situations in which it is prohibited by custom).

Why joking is illegal when you are being searched is not entirely clear to me, but that is only one of several mysteries surrounding this law. Does the law distinguish, for example, between good jokes and bad jokes? (Six months for a good one, two years for a bad one?) I don't know. But even more important, how would one know when something is a joke at all? Is there a legal definition of a joke? Suppose, while being searched, I mention that my middle name is Milton (which it is) and that I come from Flushing (which I do). I can tell you from experience that people of questionable intelligence sometimes find those names extremely funny, and it is not impossible that a few of them are airport employees. If that were the case, what would be my legal status? I have said something that has induced laughter in another. Have I, therefore, told a joke? Or look at it from the opposite view: Suppose that, upon being searched, I launch into a story about a funny thing that happened to me while boarding a plane in Chicago, concluding by saying, "And then the pilot said, 'That was no stewardess. That was my wife.'" Being of questionable intelligence myself, I think it is a hilarious story, but the guard does not. If he does not laugh, have I told a joke? Can a joke be a story that does *not* make people laugh?

It can, of course, if someone of authority says so. For the point is that in every situation, including this one, someone (or some group) has a decisive power of definition. In fact, to have power means to be able to define and to make it stick. As between the guard at the airport and me, he will have the power, not me, to define what a joke is. If his definition places me in jeopardy, I can, of course, argue my case at a trial, at which either a judge or a jury will then have the decisive authority to define whether or not my words qualified as a joke. But it is also worth noting that even if I confine my joke-telling to dinner parties, I do not escape the authority of definition. For at parties, popular opinion will decide whether or not my jokes are good ones, or even jokes at all. If opinion runs against me, the penalty is that I am not invited to many parties. There is, in short, no escaping the jurisdiction of definitions. Social order requires that there be authoritative definitions, and though you may search from now to doomsday, you will find no system without official definitions and authoritative sources to enforce them. And so we must add to the questions we ask of definition, What is the source of power that enforces the definition? And we may add further the question of what happens when those with the power to enforce definitions go mad. Here is an example that came from the Prague government several years ago. I have not made this up and produce it without further comment:

Because Christmas Eve falls on a Thursday, the day has been designated a Saturday for work purposes. Factories will close all day, with stores open a half day only. Friday, December 25, has been designated a Sunday, with both factories and stores open all day. Monday, December 28, will be a Wednesday for work purposes. Wednesday, December 30, will be a business Friday. Saturday, January 2, will be a Sunday, and Sunday, January 3, will be a Monday.

As for metaphor, I pass along a small assignment which I. A. Richards used on an occasion when I attended a seminar he conducted. (It is but one of a hundred ways to introduce the subject.) Richards divided the class into three groups. Each group was asked to write a paragraph describing language.

However, Richards provided each group with its first sentence. Group A had to begin with "Language is like a tree"; Group B with "Language is like a river"; Group C with "Language is like a building." You can imagine, I'm sure, what happened. The paragraphs were strikingly different, with one group writing of roots and branches and organic growth; another of tributaries, streams, and even floods; another of foundations, rooms, and sturdy structures. In the subsequent discussion, we did not bother with the question, Which is the "correct" description? Our discussion centered on how metaphors control what we say, and to what extent what we say controls what we see.

As I have said, there are hundreds of ways to study the relationship between language and reality, and I could go on at interminable length with ideas on how to get into it. Instead, I will confine myself to three further suggestions. The first is, simply, that the best book I know for arousing interest in the subject is Helen Keller's *The Story of My Life*. It is certainly the best account we have—from the inside, as it were—of how symbols and the abstracting process work to create a world.

Second, I would propose that in every subject—from history to biology to mathematics—students be taught, explicitly and systematically, the universe of discourse that comprises the subject. Each teacher would deal with the structure of questions, the process of definition, and the role of metaphor as these matters are relevant to his or her particular subject. Here I mean, of course, not merely what are the questions, definitions, and metaphors of a subject but also *how* these are formed and how they have been formed in the past.

Of special importance are the ways in which the forms of questions have changed over time and how these forms vary from subject to subject. The idea is for students to learn that the terminology of a question determines the terminology of its answer; that a question cannot be answered unless there are procedures by which reliable answers can be obtained; and that the value of a question is determined not only by the specificity and richness of the answers it produces but also by the quantity and quality of the new questions it raises.

Once this topic is opened, it follows that some attention must be given to how such terms as *right, wrong, truth,* and *falsehood* are used in a subject, as well as what assumptions they are based upon. This is particularly important, since words of this type cause far more trouble in students' attempts to understand a field of knowledge than do highly technical words. It is peculiar, I think, that of all the examinations I have ever seen, I have never come across one in which students were asked to say what is the basis of "correctness" or "falsehood" in a particular subject. Perhaps this is because teachers believe the issue is too obvious for discussion or testing. If so, they are wrong. I have found that students at all levels rarely have thought about the meaning of such terms in relation to a subject they are studying. They simply do not know in what sense an historical fact is different from a biological fact, or a mathematical "truth" is different from the "truth" of a literary work. Equally astonishing is that students, particularly those in elementary and secondary schools, rarely can express an intelligible sentence on the uses of the word *theory*. Since most subjects studied in school consist largely of theories, it is difficult to imagine exactly what students are in fact studying when they do their history, biology, economics, physics, or whatever. It is obvious, then, that language education must include not only the serious study of what truth and falsehood mean in the context of a subject but also what is meant by a theory, a fact, an inference, an assumption, a judgment, a generalization.

In addition, some attention must obviously be given to the style and tone of the language in a given subject. Each subject is a manner of speaking and writing. There is a rhetoric of knowledge, a characteristic way in which arguments, proofs, speculations, experiments, polemics, even humor, are expressed. One might even say that speaking or writing a subject is a performing art, and each subject requires a somewhat different kind of performance from every other. Historians, for example, do not speak or write the way biologists do. The differences have much to do with the kind of material they are dealing with, the degree of precision their generalizations permit, the type of facts they marshal, the traditions of their subject, the type of training they receive, and the purposes for which they are making their inquiries. The rhetoric of knowledge is not an easy matter to go into, but it is worth remembering that some scholars—one thinks of Veblen in sociology, Freud in psychology, Galbraith in economics—have exerted influence as much through their manner as their matter. The point is that knowledge is a form of literature, and the various styles of knowledge ought to be studied and discussed.

What we are after here is to tell the story of language as an act of creation. This is what Socrates meant when he said, "When the mind is thinking, it is talking to itself." Twenty-five hundred years later, the great German philologist Max Müller said the same: ". . . thought cannot exist without signs, and our most important signs are words." In between, Hobbes, Locke, and Kant said the same thing. So did Bertrand Russell, Werner Heisenberg, Benjamin Lee Whorf, I. A. Richards, Alfred Korzybski, and everyone else who has thought about the matter, including Marshall McLuhan.

McLuhan comes up here because he is associated with the phrase "the extensions of man." And my third and final suggestion has to do with inquiries into the ways in which humans have extended their capacities to "bind" time and control space. I am referring to what may be called "technology education." It is somewhat embarrassing that this needs to be proposed as an innovation in schools, since Americans never tire of telling themselves that they have created a technological society. They even seem to be delighted about this and many of them believe that the pathway to a fulfilling life is through continuous technological change. One would expect then that technology education would be a familiar subject in American schools. But it is not. Technology may have entered the schools but *not* technology education. Those who doubt my contention might ask themselves the following questions: Does the average high school or college graduate know where the alphabet comes from, something of its development, and *anything* about its psychic and social effects? Does he or she know anything about illuminated manuscripts, about the origin of the printing press and its role in reshaping Western culture, about the origins of newspapers and magazines? Do our students know where clocks, telescopes, microscopes, X rays, and computers come from? Do they have any idea about how such technologies have changed the economic, social, and political life of Western culture? Could they say who Morse, Daguerre, Bell, Edison, Marconi, De Forest, Zworykin, Pulitzer, Hearst, Eisenstein, and Von Neumann were? After all, we might say these men invented the technological society. Is it too much to expect that those who live in such a society will know about them and what they thought they were creating?

I realize I am beginning to sound like E. D. Hirsch, Jr., but I find it truly astonishing that the great story of humanity's perilous and exciting romance with technology is not told in our schools. There is certainly no shortage of writers on the subject. McLuhan, while an important contributor, was neither the first nor necessarily the best who has addressed the issue of how we become what we make. One thinks, for example, of Martin Heidegger, Lewis Mumford, Jacques Ellul, Paul Goodman, Walter Ong, Walter Benjamin, Elizabeth Eisenstein, Alvin Toffler, Theodore Roszak, Norbert Wiener, Sherry Turkle, Joseph Weizenbaum, Seymour Papert, and Herbert Schiller. One may also find ideas about the subject in the "science fiction" writers I have previously alluded to— Huxley, Orwell, and Bradbury, for example. It would seem that everywhere one turns these days, there are books, articles, films, and television shows on the subject of how our technology has remade the world, and continues to remake it. It is among the leading topics of everyday conversation, especially among academics. There is, for example, hardly a school superintendent anywhere, or a college dean, who cannot give us a ready-made sermon on how we now live in an "information age." Then why do we not have a subject in which students address such questions as these: How does information differ in symbolic form? How are ideographs different from letters? How are images different from words? Paintings from photographs? Speech from writing? Television from books? Radio from television? Information comes in many forms, and at different velocities and in different quantities. Do the differences matter? Do the differences have varying psychic and social effects? The questions are almost endless. This is a serious subject.

I do not know the reasons why there is no such subject in most schools, although I have one suspect under surveillance. It is that educators confuse the teaching of how to use technology with technology education. No objection can be raised against students' learning how to use television and movie cameras, Xerox machines, and computers. (I most certainly believe students ought to be taught how to use the alphabet.)

I have no intention of quarrelling with Seymour Papert, Bill Gross, or Alan Kay about the possibility that the intelligent use of computer technology can increase students' competence in mathematics or stimulate their interest in other subjects. And I endorse those attempts (for example, in New Mexico) to have students make their own television programs so that they will gain insights into the technical problems involved. These are not trivial matters, but they are only a small part of the way in which I define technology education. As I see it, the subject is mainly about how television and movie cameras, Xerox machines, and computers reorder our psychic habits, our social relations, our political ideas, and our moral sensibilities. It is about how the meanings of information and education change as new technologies intrude upon a culture, how the meanings of truth, law, and intelligence differ among oral cultures, writing cultures, printing cultures, electronic cultures. Technology education is not a technical subject. It is a branch of the humanities. Technical knowledge can be useful, but one does not need to know the physics of television to study the social and political effects of television. One may not own an automobile, or even know how to drive one, but this is no obstacle to observing what the automobile has done to American culture.

It should also be said that technology education does not imply a negative attitude toward technology. It does imply a critical attitude. To be "against technology" makes no more sense than to be "against food." We can't live without either. But to observe that it is dangerous to eat too much food, or to eat food that has no nutritional value, is not to be "antifood." It is to suggest what may be the best uses of food. Technology education aims at students' learning about what technology helps us to do and what it hinders us from doing; it is about how technology uses us, for good or ill, and about how it has used people in the past, for good or ill. It is about how technology creates new worlds, for good or ill.

But let us assume that we may overcome any obstacles to making the story of technology a core subject in schools. What is it we would want students to know? Well, for one thing, we would want them to know the answers to all the questions I have cited. But in addition, I would include the following ten principles.

1. All technological change is a Faustian bargain. For every advantage a new technology offers, there is always a corresponding disadvantage.

2. The advantages and disadvantages of new technologies are never distributed evenly among the population. This means that every new technology benefits some and harms others.

3. Embedded in every technology there is a powerful idea, sometimes two or three powerful ideas. Like language itself, a technology predisposes us to favor and value certain perspectives and accomplishments and to subordinate others. Every technology has a philosophy, which is given expression in how the technology makes people use their minds, in what it makes us do with our bodies, in how it codifies the world, in which of our senses it amplifies, in which of our emotional and intellectual tendencies it disregards.

4. A new technology usually makes war against an old technology. It competes with it for time, attention, money, prestige, and a "worldview."

5. Technological change is not additive; it is ecological. A new technology does not merely add something; it changes everything.

6. Because of the symbolic forms in which information is encoded, different technologies have different *intellectual* and *emotional* biases.

7. Because of the accessibility and speed of their information, different technologies have different *political* biases.

8. Because of their physical form, different technologies have different *sensory* biases.

9. Because of the conditions in which we attend to them, different technologies have different *social* biases.

10. Because of their technical and economic structure, different technologies have different *content* biases.

All of these principles being deeply, continuously, and historically investigated by students, I would then propose the following final examination, which is in two parts.

Part I: Choose one pre–twentieth century technology—for example, the alphabet, the printing press, the telegraph, the factory—and indicate what were the main intellectual, social, political, and economic advantages of the technology, and why. Then indicate what were the main intellectual, social, political, and economic disadvantages of the technology, and why.

Part II: Indicate, first, what you believe are or will be the main advantages of computer technology, and why; second, indicate what are or will be the main disadvantages of computer technology, and why.

Any student who can pass this examination will, I believe, know something worthwhile. He or she will also have a sense of how the world was made and how it is being remade, and may even have some ideas on how it *should* be remade.

Epilogue

The title of my book was carefully chosen with a view toward its being an ambiguous prophecy. As I indicated at the start, *The End of Education* could be taken to express a severe pessimism about the future. But if you have come this far, you will know that the book itself refuses to accept such a future. I have tried my best to locate, explain, and elaborate narratives that may give nontrivial purposes to schooling, that would contribute a spiritual and serious intellectual dimension to learning. But I must acknowledge—here in my final pages—that I am not terribly confident that any of these will work.

Let me be clear on this point. I would not have troubled anyone—least of all, written a book—if I did not think these ideas have strength and usefulness. But the ideas rest on several assumptions which American culture is now beginning to question. For example, everything in the book assumes that the idea of "school" itself will endure. It also assumes that the idea of a "public school" is a good thing. And even further, it assumes that the idea of "childhood" still exists.

As to the first point, there is more talk than ever about schools' being nineteenth-century inventions that have outlived their usefulness. Schools are expensive; they don't do what we expect of them; their functions can be served by twenty-first-century technology. Anyone who wants to give a speech on this subject will draw an audience, and an attentive one. An even bigger audience can be found for a talk on the second point: that the idea of a "*public* school" is irrelevant in the absence of the idea of a public; that is, Americans are now so different from each other, have so many diverse points of view, and such special group grievances that there can be no common vision or unifying principles. On the last point, while writing this book, I have steadfastly refused to reread or even refer to one of my earlier books in which I claimed that childhood is disappearing. I proceeded as if this were not so. But I could not prevent myself from being exposed to other gloomy news, mostly the handwriting on the wall. Can it be true, as I read in *The New York Times*, that every day 130,000 children bring deadly weapons to school, and not only in New York, Chicago, and Detroit but in many venues thought to provide our young with a more settled and humane environment in which to grow? Can it be true, as some sociologists claim, that by the start of the twenty-first century, close to 60 percent of our children will be raised in single-parent homes? Can it be true that sexual activity (and sexual diseases) among the young has increased by 300 percent in the last twenty years? It is probably not necessary for me to go on with the "can it be true's?." Everyone agrees and all signs point to the fact that American culture is not presently organized to promote the idea of childhood; and without that idea schooling loses much of its point.

These are realistic worries and must raise serious doubts for anyone who wishes to say something about schooling. Nonetheless, I offer this book in good faith, if not as much confidence as one would wish. My faith is that school will endure since no one has invented a better way to introduce the young to the world of learning; that the public school will endure since no one has invented a better way to create a public; and that childhood will survive because without it we must lose our sense of what it means to be an adult.

Notes

Chapter 1   The Necessity of Gods

1. Eric Hoffer, *The Ordeal of Change* (New York: Harper & Row), 62.

2. Quoted in Rollo May, *The Cry for Myth* (New York: Norton), 57.

3. Quoted in "The West's Deepening Culture Crisis," *The Futurist*, November–December 1993, 12.

4. Quoted in Shlain Leonard, *Art & Physics: Parallel Visions in Space, Time and Light.* (New York: William Morrow), 430.

5. Gary Krist, "Tragedyland," *New York Times*, November 27, 1993, 19.

6. See the February 18 and 25, 1915, issues of *The Nation*. The articles were written by Horace Kallen.

Chapter 2   Some Gods That Fail

1. Quoted in *Prognosis* 16, no. 3 (August 6, 1993): 4.

2. John T. Bruer, "The Mind's Journey from Novice to Expert," *American Educator*, Summer 1993, 6–7.

3. Theodore Roszak, *The Cult of Information: The Folklore of Computers and the True Art of Thinking* (New York: Pantheon), 62–63.

4. For a full analysis of this point, see the work of Henry Levin of Stanford University.

5. See Robert J. Samuelson, "The Useless 'Jobs Summit,' " *Newsweek*, March 14, 1994, 50.

6. *New York Times*, February 23, 1994, B7.

7. "Tying Education to the Economy." *New York Times*, February 20, 1994, 21.

Chapter 3   Some New Gods That Fail

1. Although I find myself reluctant to accept such studies, there are three or four that claim that when hospitalized patients are prayed for (without their knowledge or the knowledge of their physicians), they tend to improve at a greater rate than those who are not prayed for. See *Healing Words* by Larry Dossey, M.D. (HarperCollins, 1993).

2. Diane Ravitch, "When School Comes to You," *The Economist*, September 11, 1993, 45–46.

3. Hugh McIntosh, *National Research Council News Report*, Summer 1993, 2.

4. Theodore Roszak, *The Cult of Information: The Folklore of Computers and the True Art of Thinking* (New York: Pantheon), x.

5. Ravitch, *The Economist*, 46.

6. See Robert Fulghum, *All I Ever Really Needed to Know I Learned in Kindergarten* (New York: Villard).

7. *New York Times*, April 12, 1994, A13.

8. H. L. Mencken, *A Mencken Chrestomathy* (Philadelphia: The Franklin Library), 334.

9. Quoted in Larry Cuban, *Teachers and Machines: The Classroom Use of Technology Since 1920* (New York: Teachers College Press), 5.

10. Warren Crichlow et al., "Multicultural Ways of Knowing: Implications for Practice," *Journal of Education*, 172, no. 2 (1990): 102.

11. Lévi-Strauss, Claude, "The Structure of Myth," in *The Structural Anthropology* (Chicago: University of Chicago Press), 119.

12. Arthur Schlesinger, Jr., *The Disuniting of America* (New York: Norton), 29–30.

13. Ibid., 94.

Chapter 4   Gods That May Serve

1. Much of this conversation has been printed in German in *Über Morgen: Das Magazin Für Reise in Die Zukunft*, Summer 1994, 12–14.

2. Jacob Bronowski, *The Ascent of Man* (Boston: Little, Brown), 374.

3. Cornel West, *Race Matters* (New York: Vintage), 159.

4. See Susanne Langer in *Feeling and Form* (New York: Scribner's).

Chapter 5   The Spaceship Earth

1. See Harvey Kantor, "Managing the Transition from School to Work: The False Promise of Youth Apprenticeship," *Teachers College Record*, 95, no. 1 (Summer 1994): 442–461.

2. Both quotes are found in James Reston, Jr., *Galileo: A Life* (New York: HarperCollins), 136, 142.

3. Quoted in Jacques Barzun, *The Culture of Desire* (Middletown, Connecticut: Wesleyan University Press), 110.

Chapter 7   The American Experiment

1. *Washington Post*, July 29, 1994, B3, col. 1.

Chapter 9   The Word Weavers/The World Makers

1. See Eva Berger, "Metaphor, Mind & Machine: An Assessment of the Sources of Metaphors of Mind in the Works of Selected Education Theorists" (Ph.D. dissertation, New York University, 1991).

2. I. A. Richards, *Interpretation in Teaching* (New York: Harcourt Brace), 384.

Index

BOOKS BY NEIL POSTMAN

"No contemporary essayist writing about American pop culture is more fun to read and more on target."—*Los Angeles Times*

CONSCIENTIOUS OBJECTIONS
*Stirring Up Trouble About Language,
Technology, and Education*

In this series of feisty and ultimately hopeful essays, readers will find themselves rethinking many of their bedrock assumptions: Should education transmit culture or defend us against it? Is technological innovation progress or a peculiarly American addiction?

Current Affairs/Science/Education/0-679-73421-X

THE DISAPPEARANCE OF CHILDHOOD

From the vogue for nubile models to the explosion in the juvenile crime rate, this modern classic of social history and media traces the precipitous decline of childhood in America today—and the corresponding threat to the notion of adulthood.

Media/Current Affairs/0-679-75166-1

THE END OF EDUCATION
Redefining the Value of School

In this provocative analysis, Neil Postman suggests that the current crisis in America's educational system derives from its failure to supply students with a unifying "narrative" like those that inspired earlier generations. Instead, today's schools promote the false "gods" of consumerism, technology, and ethnic separatism.

Education/0-679-75031-2

TECHNOPOLY
The Surrender of Culture to Technology

Postman launches a trenchant warning against the tyranny of machines over man in the late twentieth century. *Technopoly* chronicles our transformation from a society that uses technology to one that is shaped by it, as it also traces its effects upon what we mean by politics, religion, intellect, history—even privacy and truth.

Current Affairs/Sociology/0-679-74540-8

Available at your local bookstore, or call toll-free to order: